COURAGE OF VOICE

EMPOWERING WOMEN
TO OPEN PROFESSIONAL DOORS

DERETTA C. RHODES, Ph.D.

13TH & JOAN

For permission requests, write to the publisher addressed "Attention: Permissions Coordinator," 205 N. Michigan Avenue, Suite #810, Chicago, IL 60601. 13th & Joan books may be purchased for educational, business or sales promotional use. For information, please email the Sales Department at sales@13thandjoan.com.

Printed in the U. S. A.

First Printing, June 2024

Library of Congress Cataloging-in-Publication Data has been applied for.

Paperback ISBN: 978-1-961863-01-9
Hardcover ISBN: 978-1-961863-00-2

Praise for *Courage of Voice: Empowering Women to Open Professional Doors*

DeRetta's passion is to cultivate and support others. I marvel in her ability to understand how another person perceives a given situation. Her approach in developing competent and resilient skills in others is her hallmark. She thrives in and does not recoil from each challenging situation. She illuminates issues and ensures that you are recognizing the correct choices. By her helping you to make those hard decisions based on a thorough understanding of what is being faced, she demonstrates that engagement and collaboration never fail you.

— Richard Gerakitis,
Retired Managing Partner, Troutman Pepper

One of the greatest professional accomplishments over the course of one's career is to watch young talent emerge and go on to achieve unparalleled success. I first met Dr. DeRetta Rhodes when she was hired as an Human Resources Manager on my team in the late 1990s. From that point forward, her skills and abilities have guided her to increasing levels of responsibility and influence in some of America's most recognized companies. What a joy to watch her ascend through various roles and eventually become the Executive Vice President and Chief Culture Officer of the Atlanta Braves. Whether in her capacity as a C-Suite executive in the male-dominated sports arena or as a board director focused on the needs of the most vulnerable among us, Dr. Rhodes brings an exceptional level of business acumen born out of decades of experience in Corporate America, rigorous academic research and study, and a genuine commitment to helping others achieve their highest vision of themselves. Simply put, DeRetta Cole Rhodes, PhD., serves as a testament to others that with hard work, perseverance, and faith, the sky is the limit.

— Rodney W. Whitmore,
Chief Human Resources Officer, Great Minds

DeRetta elevates others by sharing her time, knowledge, and resources willingly. She impacts her community with her years of corporate leadership experience and relentless pursuit of excellence. Her actions are a beautiful example of what you can achieve when you work tirelessly to achieve your goals. She has boldly and unapologetically surpassed the expectations of naysayers. She has taught me the power of standing up for yourself and using your voice. I can't think of anyone better to write a book about encouraging and empowering women in the workplace.

— Cheryl Polote Williamson,
CEO and Founder, Williamson Media Group; Author

DeRetta is an inspiring leader who builds trust with peers, partners, and teammates by genuinely investing herself in others' success. Building trust, along with her grit, perseverance and "can-do" attitude have enabled her to deliver impressive outcomes. Her personal commitment to deliver despite barriers and obstacles has catapulted her into the C-Suite and literally into the major league.

— Barry C. McCarthy,
President and CEO, Deluxe Corporation

To *everyone*...always use your *voice*.

They told me I couldn't.
That's why I did.

ACKNOWLEDGMENTS

FIRST, I GIVE HONOR TO GOD WHO IS THE CENTER OF MY LIFE. MY parents and grandparents gave me that foundation that has always allowed me to be centered with all that I do.

To my amazing husband, best friend, and soulmate, Leon Rhodes. You have been my rock and provided me unwavering support in all that I do. You allow me to dream, worry, and everything in between, with no judgment. You are my person!

To my sons Cole, Austin, and Jordan. I always want to make you each proud.

To my parents, DeRay and Fay Cole. Because of your relentless pursuit of knowledge, you have instilled in me the constant desire of learning and education. I hope that I am able to provide the wisdom and grace that you have provided to me.

To my brother Andre'. You were there from the beginning and always make me feel like I am 10 feet tall.

To my amazing village of friends, mentors, sponsors, and supporters who have held me up through every step. I owe each of you my appreciation and gratitude.

And lastly, my author coach, Susan Blystone. I appreciate you beyond belief. You kept me on schedule and on the timeline I created. This book would still be in my head if not for your conversations, texts, and relentless pursuit to keep me on task and achieve my dream of becoming an author.

CONTENTS

INTRODUCTION

DEAR READER:

I am writing to you from the C-Suite, not to boast but rather to empower and encourage you by sharing the rough road I traveled to get from paycheck to position. I've been denied opportunities and passed over for promotions. While some doors were unlocked as I progressed in my career, many more were slammed tightly shut. I had to obtain the key to remove the barrier, an often-complicated task that required I gain courage of voice.

And still, the setbacks continued. I've been laid off. I've endured microaggressions and blatant attacks. I have had to fight for salary equity as most women do, but nothing has deterred me from continuing, rising, and thriving.

The reality is that I knew when I walked in the room that those present only saw a Black female—not my aspirations, goals, talents, motivations, achievements, or passions. At every meeting I heard repeated in my head the words spoken to me at various stages of my life: *You are not capable of being a leader. You will not graduate with your Ph.D. Who do you think you are to be in a C-Suite position?*

I have fought against all the stigmas that came with the labels, enduring pain that ran long and deep. I became a divorced, single mother of two sons at the age of 38. It took me seven years to complete my doctorate. I must often remind people that I did not pursue a doctorate so that you could call me "Doctor," but so that I could have credibility when sitting at the table.

The fear and isolation were often crippling as I continued my journey. The naysayers and cynics were always present. And yet, I have been blessed to advance my career at various corporations and agencies, rising from a director to a vice president then senior vice president. I currently serve as Executive Vice President and Chief Culture Officer for the Atlanta Braves.

My priority has always been to avoid becoming bitter or angry when facing challenges directly linked to my gender or race. I channel all negative energy into a positive outcome, which is one reason I authored this book. I consequently share my story openly, vulnerably, and unapologetically.

The journey chronicled in the following pages may evoke sadness or joy. My goal is that you gain revelation and hope as I did while walking through the fire thanks in large part to the most amazing support and love from the tribe that I embraced through the years.

Join me as I dissect my story of expectations realized through perseverance. I hope that when you complete reading, you will realize that we all have a story that needs to be told. May our truth create a road map for those still struggling to find their voice, open doors, and fulfill their dreams.

DeRetta Rhodes

1

UNDERSTANDING THE DYNAMIC

As a third-generation college graduate in a Black family, I was blessed to be raised in a home where questioning, discussing, dissecting, and debating issues was the norm. What was felt in the heart was inevitably analyzed by the head, meaning emotion was countered by intellect. It was consequently not surprising that when I experienced painful isolation during the early years of my career as a Black woman in the business world, I was motivated to delve into the reasons why. I knew the immediate and obvious answer: In most employment situations, I have been the only Black woman in a room of all white men and some white women. I have consistently and unfortunately felt like the token employee who checked two boxes as a minority female.

Instead of succumbing to this negative self-perception, I opted to study what I was experiencing in the workplace. I spent months examining how racism and sexism impact the career progression of executive Black women in U.S. corporations while earning my doctorate at the University of Georgia. For my dissertation, I completed a qualitative study titled "Courage Under Fire: How Black Women Have Learned to Survive in Corporate America." I surveyed and interviewed Black women working for Fortune 500 organizations as directors or vice presidents. I wanted to know their experiences, hear their responses to difficult professional situations, and embrace their wisdom as mentors who had achieved a career pinnacle I was determined to reach.

Before gaining their insights, I needed to better understand the broad corporate dynamic Black women encounter in the 21st century. Researching the subject made me quickly realize that being the only one and feeling isolated from your peers or staff in the workplace is a reality every Black woman faces because of her gender and race. Those who aspire to leadership roles quickly encounter tokenism, dualism, and assimilation challenges that become a burdensome weight they carry on their ascent to positions of power.

Tokenism refers to the way in which a minority person is labeled as the only one in a group. It allows organizations to say that they value diversity because they have one or two minority employees. The negative impact of tokenism is conveyed vividly by Judith Turnock and Price Cobbs, who authored the book *Cracking the Corporate Code: The Revealing Success Stories of 32 African-American Executives*. They discovered that "in every relationship throughout the organization, being a Black American is a salient feature. There are times you feel uncomfortably visible, as if in a fishbowl. At other times, you feel you are not seen at all. Not very long ago—not even two generations—each Black in Corporate America was in fact isolated as 'the first' and 'the only.'"

Dualism is an equally difficult dynamic to overcome. It occurs when Black women find that they must exist in different cultures, which forces them to juggle alternate lives. They work, live, worship, and socialize in unique spaces that typically require them to show different aspects of who they are as a person compared to how they present themselves in the corporation. The end result is that Black women become increasingly stressed as they straddle the cultural line that separates where they live from where they work. Myriad studies confirm that Black women are pressured to fit into the separate dichotomies of their personal and professional cultures. Because there is very little integration with such cultural pluralism, they consequently often create distinct lives while struggling with their core identity.

Knowing who they are is consequently a constant challenge for Black women in Corporate America because of the need to assimilate to their work environment. By definition, assimilation is losing oneself in the environment that you are a part of. It can be argued that assimilating into an organization is the best way to rise to an executive level. But doing so incurs a personal cost for professional gain because assimilation requires that Black women leave a part of their own culture behind. They all too often may lose who they are, especially if they do not identify with the corporate culture. An equally significant problem with assimilation is that the goal is to make racial differences irrelevant, meaning the uniqueness Black women bring to an organization is not celebrated or appreciated but instead intentionally suppressed.

There is the further complication of the glass ceiling that is always present, a reality made obvious by the fact there are few

Black women in executive positions within corporations. They are also consistently absent in the boardroom where critical decisions are being made. This is an inevitable reality given the number of Black women in executive positions as compared to the population is disproportionate. When my dissertation was published in 2010, the U.S. Equal Employment Opportunity Commission reported that there were 3.7 million women of color in the United States workforce. Black women represented 8 percent of America's private-sector workforce and a mere 1.1 percent of corporate officers in Fortune 500 companies. More recently, CNN did a news story in February 2021 about Black executive women making history in the C-Suite. The report revealed that in 2018, only 3.3 percent of all U.S. corporate executives were filled by Black people. At the time of that news coverage, only two Black women were CEOs.

These discouraging numbers lead me to agree with those who argue the corporate ceiling Black women hit should more accurately be called concrete versus glass because the chance of penetrating into executive ranks is as difficult as blasting through cement. "Despite the progress made in the workplace by women and minorities in recent years, it is quite apparent that there remains a great disparity in the executive suite of Corporate America. Women and minorities are greatly under-represented in executive roles at major American companies," Northern Illinois University Senior Research Associate Patricia Inman concluded in her article "Women's career development at the glass ceiling."

The odds of arriving in the C-Suite are low for Black women because they are ostracized by the mere design of Corporate America. The blueprint for how corporations function was drawn up decades ago by white, mainstream males who created an elitist culture and structure. Racism, higher expectations, exclusion and isolation—as well as a lack of company commitment to advancement—keep the ceiling in place. Black women consequently find themselves in "racialized positions" that are not mainstream roles, do not wield power, and do not nurture employees aspiring to lead.

Just as there are impeding preconceptions about race that require an ongoing battle against the stereotype of the deficient Black woman, there is also the archaic mindset of too many male bosses who question a woman's ambition, commitment, and ability to lead simply because of her additional roles as wife or mother. Both are obstacles Black women must overcome, as documented by scholars Katherine Giscombe and Mary Mathis in a *Journal of Business Ethics* article titled "Leveling the playing field for women of color in corporate management: Is the business case enough?" Their multi-phased research study concluded that "Black women are increasingly being hired in management positions, which means that major barriers to upward mobility are no longer at the recruitment and job entry stages of employment, but at the advancement stages."

In light of this reality, it is not surprising that Black women develop the perspective that they must out-learn, out-pace, and out-do all of their contemporary counterparts, as noted by wellness coach Yoji Cole in an article published by *DiversityInc* magazine. That mindset is all too often embraced as the safety harness for Black women aspiring to climb higher within a corporation. Their unique challenge, as identified by Dr. Kecia Thomas, is "developing a healthy and positive identity within an environment that often portrays their racial groups quite negatively and uniformly." Thomas, who shares this perspective in her book titled *Diversity Dynamics in the Workplace*, is an expert scholar on the psychology of workplace diversity and serves as dean of the College of Arts and Sciences at the University of Alabama at Birmingham.

Given this historical context and current paradigm for Corporate America, it makes sense that Black women feel isolated and alienated as they strive to prove their worth to the corporation—all while dodging political landmines as they work to penetrate the leadership circle. Their struggle is perhaps best understood through the lens of Critical Race Feminism, which provides a platform for dissecting the challenging corporate experiences tied to race and gender that Black women encounter. Based on legal discourse, Critical Race Feminism posits that race and gender are embedded in all that is experienced by Black women. The need to focus on both is summarized succinctly by Adrien Wing, director of the University of Iowa Center for Human Rights and professor in the university's College of Law. She makes the argument that to truly understand what Black women face in their professional world requires viewing both their gender and race. "Their identities must be multiplied together to create a holistic one when analyzing the nature of the discrimination against them," Wing states in the book of essays titled *Critical Race Feminism*, which she edited.

Race and gender shape the experiences that Black women face because both are a permanence of who they are. The duality they juggle in the many different roles that they play in their homes, communities, organizations, and corporations speaks to their complexity. Critical Race Feminism allows a framework for acknowledging both race and gender when dissecting complex issues and challenges because it creates an intersection of Critical Race Theory and Black Feminism. It further acknowledges that racism and gender are endemic to American culture and society.

Critical Race Feminism is the ideal analytical tool to better comprehend how society exists along the lines of hierarchy that include race and gender. With regard to my doctoral work, the theory was a lens to dissect how Black women exist in Corporate America. The understanding gained through Critical Race Feminism relies on storytelling and narratives from women of color who have traditionally been oppressed. This includes Black women in Corporate America who must move beyond concerns of silence and authority to ensure that their voices are heard.

It takes courage for a Black woman to find her voice in Corporate America for reasons already explored. The isolation, identity angst, and roadblocks to advancement instill insecurity versus fuel the inner strength needed to challenge the oppressive culture. The reality is that Black women often struggle just to complete their education and find their way to a job before they can even begin building a career. Their professional development is frequently overshadowed by the fact that they are the family's major breadwinner. Their primary goal is consequently to pay the bills and provide financial security for their children. The work of researcher Joann Cohn emphasizes that the priority of meeting basic family needs comes into play long before Black women begin to contemplate pursuing their career goals that often seem far beyond reach.

Those who are able to pivot their focus to professional aspirations must take inventory of the inevitable personal and professional challenges yet to come. They must seek to become empowered, which is yet another difficult task because Black women in Corporate America are typically denied access to executives, mentoring, assignments with high visibility, and minority role models. Attempts to build informal networks result in additional frustration. Individuals tend to gravitate toward others who look like themselves, yet there are very few Black women in executive ranks. Even when such a group is identified and a social connection established, opportunities to connect are frequently missed. Because of the responsibilities Black women hold beyond work in their home and community, they are often not available for the golf outing or happy hour. Remember that these additional roles are largely in place because of how Black women have been historically socialized within their families and by society in general. Attending to other tasks means that in the corporate world, isolation and the status quo continue because Black women are unable to create relationships of trust that are vital to career advancement.

Even having exceptional credentials, academic degrees, and an impressive resume may not be enough for the Black woman to scale the corporate ladder because she is always judged by a very different standard than her white counterpart. Experience and knowledge are weighed against the stereotype of incompetence, a reality explored by professors Ella Edmondson Bell and Stelle Nkomo who study issues facing women in management. It is no wonder given such an oppressive environment that Black women frequently become a shadow in corporations. For many, silence is a form of protection. It is also a detriment to learning and represents a loss of power. It is consequently essential for Black women to find the courage needed to use their voices and tell their stories of professional struggles if Corporate America is ever going to change.

My dissertation became a platform for 11 Black women in a leadership position within a Fortune 500 company for more than five years to tell of their journey to the C-Suite. Participants all held at least a bachelor's degree, led a team of employees, and were older than 30. Each submitted a resume and participated in an interview that centered on two key questions: What are the significant learning experiences that supported Black women's career progression in Corporate America? What strategies have Black women used to support their career progression in Corporate America? The data revealed four themes: Negotiating an unwelcomed existence, battling ethgender isolation in Corporate America, serving as a domestic in the corporate boardroom, and creating strategies from lessons learned.

Each participant in the study revealed that they carried a racial consciousness that made them aware they were unwelcome. They all readily spoke of the impact racism and sexism had on their career, saying that they believed their work was either not recognized or perceived as deficient. They consequently felt overworked, underappreciated, and marginalized. As a result, each experienced loneliness and expressed how they felt compelled to always outperform their white female counterparts. It was not unusual for there to be feelings of hostility, as one participant explained in describing an ongoing battle with colleagues:

> Oftentimes, I felt like I may be in warfare. And with that warfare came day-to-day combat that could be both rewarding but exhausting. I say rewarding because oftentimes, I was the only Black female in many of the meetings that I participated in, and I felt like it was an obligation that I must fulfill to be a voice in the room. But in the same instance, it often felt like battle fatigue because there is always a fight and there is always a scrimmage that I had to fight and that could become very tiring. But the reality is that you have to always be battle-ready.

The second theme that emerged also tied to the first research question regarding learning experiences as the Black women progressed to leadership roles in Corporate America. While none of the study's participants were proclaimed feminists,

11

each believed in fairness and equal access. Each was attracted to the corporate world because they felt confident the American dream awaited them. Unfortunately, each quickly realized that they are forever viewed differently from men and from white colleagues. Their lack of race and gender privilege defined their corporate experiences. Each emphasized feeling isolated as the only Black female in the room and being subjected to different scrutiny than their white female counterparts. Each participant shared the struggle of blaming themselves and self-deprecation that inevitably surfaced as they attempted to be loyal to a corporation in which they felt ostracized. Instead of scrutinizing the environment and realizing the fatal flaws, they placed an onus on themselves to overcome obstacles.

To counter feeling vulnerable, these Black women developed a game plan to always be more prepared than their white counterparts. As one executive stated: "I feel that I have had to break down barriers. Being the only one has been very difficult because they view me differently when I walk in the room. I have to ensure that I have more education, more licensing, just more than my counterparts. I had to make sure that I was very polite and got along with people because I did not want to be viewed as the angry Black woman. I constantly feel like I have to fight that perception, and I am always proving myself."

Answers to the second question regarding strategies these Black women developed to survive in Corporate America were equally revealing and troubling. As the first generation to tackle top executive roles, they had no role models or roadmap to guide their trajectory. They consequently duplicated adapting methods that have worked for them as a member of the disenfranchised group in other settings. Each reported a strategy of doing grunt work or tackling projects, positions, and assignments that were more difficult or less desirable with the goal of proving themselves in order to obtain future opportunities. One negative result of that approach is that each reported feeling that they served as the domestic in the boardroom.

Functioning from a subservient role meant these Black women were not seen as worthy professionals with credentials, talents, and achievements on par or above that of their white female peers. "It was as if I was going to boot camp with every new assignment and role that they threw at me with no recognition of what I had done previously," one of the women shared. "In my mind, as a Black female, your leadership is more of being a servant to the company that you serve." Another participant stated, "I get tired of being the maid that does the clean-up work but am not recognized for what I bring to the table."

Given such a hostile dynamic, each woman reported having to create strategies to survive against the odds and successfully reach higher echelons of the corporation. They did so through self-awareness, mentoring, networking, and performance. Knowing yourself and staying grounded in your truth was deemed essential to advancing in Corporate America. As one participant stated: "Oftentimes, you may be the only female in the room, and certainly the only Black female. And you may feel compelled to just 'fit in.' Your confidence may be construed as arrogance; your strength might be construed as overbearing. But never back down to your thoughts, beliefs, and opinions because you will regret it later." Another noted that every situation provides something instructive or reveals an aspect of who you are. She advised to "always reflect to see if the who you are at a given time matches who you want to be."

Mentoring is essential for Black women to succeed in Corporate America. Each person in the study emphasized the need to find someone within the organization and someone external who they could speak to in trust and receive candid guidance. The mentor gives objective feedback, providing tools and suggestions for navigating the corporate culture and dealing with specific personalities. "Everyone needs a champion to help them maneuver and work through their career," one woman in the study said, summarizing the invaluable role a mentor has in empowering Black women as they navigate the maze within Corporate America. All of the women also noted the need for themselves to serve as a mentor who willingly lifts up the younger Black women still struggling on their career path.

Networking complements the benefits of mentoring. Establishing relationships within the corporation and externally provides exposure to a variety of people with differing experiences and knowledge. The women also advised making connections beyond their specific work unit or department within the company, as well as broadly in their profession through industry associations and memberships. Having an established network brings the "big picture" perspective to each individual situation, allowing for a growing sense of self-value. Another positive is that employment opportunities often surface through other professionals within the network.

Ultimately, the ability to survive in Corporate America comes down to consistently performing at a high level. Each of the Black women interviewed emphasized the need to focus on executing exceptionally well in their current position in order to be considered for advancement. "You will need to be so much better than others that you work with," one participant stated. "You may resent it but accept it. If it becomes unbearable, look for employment elsewhere. Be prepared to accept any promotion offered because you may not be offered another promotional opportunity. Employers don't like rejection any more than individuals do."

The harsh realities exposed from the research done for my dissertation were disheartening yet uplifting. The significant challenges exposed by the Black women were daunting, however, their candor created a sense of camaraderie that was comforting given I was not an outsider in the study. I was instead an active participant with a similar story to tell. Remember that I was working in Human Resources while completing my doctorate. I had my own moment of cognitive dissonance in the workplace when I realized that I would never become a vice president at the organization I had been a part of for more than five years. The lack of advancement was not because I did not possess the skills or needed additional education. I was convinced it was instead because I am a Black woman.

The work done for my dissertation not only confirmed my suspicions about my own career struggles but fueled my ambition to overcome the odds and make it to the C-Suite. I felt empowered given the insights and advice I gleaned from interacting with the women who participated in the research. They candidly revealed how they found a way to survive in Corporate America despite never feeling they were part of the work environment where they consistently battled racism and sexism. Although each one expressed their level of discomfort in corporate roles that frequently relegated them to servitude, these Black women found ways to turn hard lessons into fodder for career growth.

I came to three conclusions after analyzing the experiences shared. One is that successful career progression forced the executive Black women in this study to learn to negotiate their tension-filled lives while constantly weighing their cultural alliances against their corporate acceptance. The second truth I gleaned is that the women used their negative racial and gendered experiences to find ways to inform and manage their careers. Finally, it became clear that these women—who described themselves as "accidental administrators"—believed they succeeded because they obeyed culturally grounded rules that mandated perseverance rather than submit to Corporate America's hostile norms of racially driven isolation, hostility, and nonacceptance.

Each of the women in my study made a poignant impression. Each was vulnerable yet brave as they discussed their experiences and how they would like to see younger Black professional women have better experiences than what they encountered and endured. Their separate yet similar hurdles and heartaches that came with the climb to professional leadership roles made clear the radical changes that need to occur in Corporate America. One way to begin the transformation is to build the promotion of minorities—and specifically Black women—into the reward system for top executives within the corporation. Another recommendation is to redistribute the power structure and set up prescribed career strategies and ladders.

Such fundamental change requires a paradigm shift that will not be achieved easily or quickly. Until that day when the dynamic is altered, Black women must continue to rely upon their stamina and wisdom to not just survive but excel. They must create for themselves a safety net of individuals who provide encouragement that in turn bolsters confidence. Each must continue to share their story as a testimony to the power that is unleashed when Black women have the courage of voice to state their reality and demonstrate their resilience.

LESSONS LEARNED

Each Black female executive I interviewed for my dissertation had survived and arrived in a position of leadership in Corporate America. I understood the fortitude needed to reach such success and appreciated every bit of wisdom they imparted. In an effort to have their voices heard and their knowledge shared, I asked them to write advice to the young Black woman motivated by similar professional aspirations but in need of guidance to overcome inevitable obstacles and achieve her goals. Following are the letters from some of the participants. Take to heart their words of wisdom and appreciate the lessons they willingly offer to make Corporate America easier for you to navigate.

PARTICIPANT 1

I am writing to you to share my perspective on establishing a career in Corporate America. Specifically, there are three items I want to highlight. They are the importance of relationships, continuous learning and finally, being your authentic self. The corporate work environment is a combination of relationships. It is essentially many relationships rolled up into one, the organization itself. And generally speaking, most individuals in an organization share the same ideals, values, and principles. These ideals translate into its "corporate culture." With that said, learning to navigate through takes time. Over the next several years, you will meet a variety of people, work with a variety of people, and share a variety of experiences. As you have interactions, keep in mind that each person possesses something unique and brings something different to the table. With that said, do not judge a book by its cover. One could have so much more to offer than what you initially think.

Also, don't burn bridges. You will not like everyone you work with and vice versa, but as hard as it is, always maintain professionalism. You never know whose path you will cross 10 years down the road. The world is a funny place and you often reconnect with people from prior times/experiences, especially in the workforce. Finally, it is just as important to connect with your peers as it is to connect with executives. We all like to befriend executives, but your peers will end up in places you would never imagine. From a personal standpoint, you should continue learning and gaining knowledge. Just because you finished college does not mean there is nothing else out there to gain. Always be in a learning mode. The day you stop learning or lack the desire to increase yourself within your work environment is the day you should walk out the door and pursue something else. You continue to learn by technical updates related to your work, joining professional associations and networking, and by building relationships with others who have expertise in areas you may not be as familiar with. Finally, always be your authentic self. Oftentimes you may be the only female in the room, and certainly the only Black female. And you may feel compelled to just "fit in." Your confidence might be construed as arrogance, your strength might be construed as overbearing, but never back down on your thoughts, beliefs, and opinions because you will regret it later. People will test you in a variety of ways simply because you don't look or act like them, or even just because you have a different perspective. What you have to understand is that the world is big enough for everyone. And although what you bring to the table may be different, it is just as valuable as what the next person brings. I hope this helps as you begin your journey. It will get rough and there could be days you will want to walk out and quit, but resist the urge if it is your passion.

PARTICIPANT 2

Beginning a career in Corporate America can be very exciting and rewarding. As you embark on your first professional role, here are a few "nuggets" to consider.

1. Focus on execution. In order for you to be considered for the next role, you need to deliver results at your current level.
2. Keep a record of all of your successes/accomplishments. You can refer to this document during your performance review or if there is an opportunity for a promotion.
3. Get to know your immediate team. Establishing strong relationships will allow you to be more productive.
4. Arrive on time to work and all meetings.
5. Dress appropriately.
6. Be passionate about your work, but keep your emotions intact when you are trying to make a point.

I hope these "nuggets" will help set a solid foundation for a successful career.

PARTICIPANT 3

My advice to you is set forth below.

1. First and foremost: Don't engage in conduct you would not want your loved ones to learn about or see in any form of media, including but not limited to the news or the front page of the *Wall Street Journal*, *New York Times*, or their local newspaper. Social networks are included. Think of the possible long-term consequences before you post material on social network sites. Forgo immediate gratification and the "knee-jerk" temptation to communicate the first thought

that comes to mind. Imagine that when you're 45 you're asked to be the CEO of a Fortune 500 company or offered a cabinet post and your loved ones, including your children, are watching the evening news when the forgotten films of your younger years are shown nationally. Ask yourself...*Is it worth it?* Let me answer for you...*No!* If you don't follow the advice, you will not be heard to complain later.

2. You will need to be so much better than others you work with. You may resent it, but accept it. If it becomes unbearable, look for employment elsewhere.

3. Respect yourself. If you don't, don't expect respect from others.

4. Do not crap where you eat. Engaging in romantic/sexual relationships at work is very risky because consensual relationships have been known to "go south." Find love/lust elsewhere, unless you are willing to risk losing your good name, reputation, and possibly your job. Having said that, if you assume the risk and find true love, one of you should leave the company to avoid possible conflicts of interest.

5. Before you leave for work, look in the mirror and ask yourself...*Is this the statement I want to make?* Personal appearance is critical. Dress for success and walk tall. You don't know who you'll meet on any given day. Remember, you only have one chance to make a first impression.

6. Seek employment with employers that encourage and value ethics and integrity and embrace those values. If after you're hired you don't believe your employer operates in accordance with those values, seek employment elsewhere. Your professional and personal reputations are your stock and trade.

7. Remember, if you are employed at will without an employment contract, no matter what they tell you, it's

your employer's party and you are merely an invited guest. Absent extenuating circumstances (often legal), you can be asked to leave, but you can choose to leave at any time.

8. When a person shows you who they are, believe them.

9. Loyalty and trust are important, but not always reciprocated. Companies are not loyal, but individuals should be. Don't "throw anyone under the bus" unless there are legal implications or you are asked a direct question that requires a direct, honest answer. Be loyal to individuals who deserve it and who are loyal to you. It helps to have a friend at work, preferably in another department.

10. Find a knowledgeable mentor and/or hire an executive coach. You'll need experience and objectivity to help you navigate corporate cultures and to deal with personalities.

11. Decide whether you want to be a leader or an individual contributor.

12. Establish attainable career goals. Develop a plan to achieve your goals and execute against your plan. A written plan will help keep you focused and let you know if you're off track. You may decide later to revise your goals and plan. As you progress professionally, your goals may change.

13. Avoid workplace disputes. If there is a dispute, "don't have a nickel in that dime" unless you feel strongly to suffer the consequences. It may cost you the promotion you were expecting or a presentation you expected to make that would have increased your visibility to executives.

14. Even if your company does a good job of career pathing and developing its employees, take responsibility for your own career. Obtaining certifications in specialized areas is good, but degrees are better. Take advantage of tuition assistance benefits, if available. Education and training will make you

more marketable and they are portable if you decide to change jobs.

15. Avoid conspicuous consumption. Managers can be petty. If you have the money to take trips and make expensive purchases, your manager may feel that you're being paid too much and give you a lower merit increase or bonus or fail to promote you.

16. Be the best employee you can be. Establish a reputation for being a reliable, punctual, flexible, detail-oriented, well-prepared, pleasant team player who can "think outside the box." Don't be a clock watcher.

17. Don't be a "schemer and a scammer," but learn to recognize those who are and try to avoid them.

18. Be prepared to accept any promotion offered because you may not be offered another promotional opportunity. Employers don't like rejection any more than individuals do.

19. If your employer has a 401(k) plan, enroll in it. You will be glad you did, and not just for retirement.

20. Keep your loved ones out of the workplace. Well-meaning significant others and parents should never call your employer on your behalf. The only exception I can think of is if you are too sick to call in to inform your supervisor that you will be absent.

21. Establish relationships outside your department and function and at various levels. It's amazing how much you can learn about the "big picture" when you talk to people who have functional responsibilities that are different from yours.

22. Be discrete and maintain confidences.

23. Never lie. No good will come of it.

24. Maintain personal financial integrity. You don't want a garnishment against your paycheck. Imagine the message that would send to your employer.
25. Give back by making charitable donations and/or donating your time. Not only is this a way to help others, it may create new contacts that will benefit you going forward.

I salute you and wish you well!

PARTICIPANT 4

So you are embarking on a corporate career. That's great! If your experience is anything like mine, then you're in for the ride of your life. I am not talking about meeting incredible people, tackling challenging projects, or engaging the world through multi-cultures, though I hope you are blessed to do all those things. I'm referring to a much more personal journey. Believe it or not, a corporate career, like any chosen profession, invites you to learn more about YOU: What motivates you, what scares you, how you relate to others, live your values, and manage your ego. So pay attention. Every situation will surface something instructive or revealing about who you are. Reflect to see if the who you are at any given time matches who you want to be. Sometimes you will be, sometimes you won't. When there is a disconnect, work to close the gap. There were times when the choices I made were not in keeping with who I wanted to be. Too many were the times I spent responding to emails instead of being fully present with family. I let work encroach on life with family, friends, or leisure pursuits. I blame no one but myself but in retrospect, I would have more closely guarded time with loved ones. No salary, level, or sphere of influence is more important than those closest to you. As a woman of faith, I thank God for the gifts that enabled my corporate success. I also thank Him for opportunities He gives to minister and be ministered to. Many days I was encouraged by colleagues and coworkers who live their faith, sometimes overtly and others simply letting their light shine. The earth is the Lord's and the fullness thereof. Praise God, this applies to corporations as well. Don't hide your faith, share it! My sister, many blessings on your career! May you experience the full breadth, depth, and scope of life in the corporate world.

PARTICIPANT 5

I've been asked to write a letter to a young Black woman who has made the decision to join Corporate America. Herein, then, what you have is some of my most urgent thoughts as it relates to succeeding both personally and professionally. In many instances, I've given you personal examples of what I mean not for you to follow but to model what I mean. First things first, start with who you are on the inside.

1. You have to have and own your own definition of success. For me, success means:
    - Growing in my walk with Christ.
    - Having a healthy, thriving marriage.
    - Being an active, involved, hands-on mom to our son.
    - Nurturing healthy relationships with my extended family and friends.
    - Doing paid and unpaid work that allows me to make meaningful contributions while simultaneously providing me with opportunities to grow my technical and functional skills.

Those are my five hallmarks of success and in that order. Once I got my heart and mind around what I wanted in terms of success, I then had to continue to define and live in a way that is consistent with how I define success:

1. Church and Sunday School on Sunday. Bible study on Wednesday. Daily devotional and prayer time.
2. Date night with my husband every Saturday night. Home-made dinner more times than not each week. Vacation with and without our son. Scheduled sex if it comes to that.
3. I have a standing date three Saturdays of each month to take my son to the zoo. The one Saturday I don't take him to the zoo is when I take my mom to our monthly spa date. My parents and my mother-in-law all live in the metro area. Friday night is family night. We eat dinner as a family. It rotates from house to house. I see my parents every day.
4. I serve on a number of nonprofit boards. My passion is the preservation of the family with a particular emphasis on the stewardship of children. That's the first filter for my involvement. My second filter is the time requirement. If the math as it relates to time doesn't work, then I can't commit to it. I have learned to say no gracefully and to offer up viable alternatives. Paid work. I am nine months into a new job. In considering the opportunity, the primary questions were: What do I have to offer? What do I stand to gain? I generally work from 9 to 6. I have a 45-minute commute each way. I don't talk on the telephone during my morning commute as that is time set aside for my son. On my evening commute, I use the time to return telephone calls, etc. I have a Blackberry, however, it rarely makes it into the house. I check it in the morning before I start my

commute and one last time before I enter my home. I have all kinds of rules with respect to how many breakfast and lunch appointments during the week, both internal and external. My goal is no more than two evening functions per week. I don't (as opposed to won't) work on weekends. I take all my vacation. I give you all that context because I genuinely believe if you don't have a general, holistic view of your entire life, you can't be successful in a sustainable way by anyone else's measure at work. A friend of mine teaches a terrific time management class in which she has participants literally map out a 24-hour period. The "aha" is the question: Is how you are spending your time reflective of what you say is important to you? For me, if I am not spending sufficient time in my five areas of "success," I know I have to recalibrate. As it relates to specific workplace tools and tips, consider the following:

a. Have at least one skill that hands down you are the best at. A demonstrated, documented competence is a must. Enthusiasm is necessary and insufficient. Complete the following sentence: "Hands down, I am the best at _____." Whatever you answered with, that is where you need to spend your energy. Hone that skill. Promote that skill. Look for opportunities to use that skill. Know the value of that skill. Know your number two and three skills as well, however, focus on your primary skill.

b. Know how you will contribute to an organization. What is your value proposition? Complete another sentence for me: "I will contribute to my employer's vision/mission by _____." We women tend to focus on what we do. That should only be half of our focus. Our full focus should be HOW what we do contributes to the success of the organizations we work for.

c. Understand your employer's economic model for making money. What does the company you plan to work for do and how will your work support the company's marketplace objectives? This is particularly true for individuals in staff positions. You don't need to become an imitation CFO. You DO have to understand the basics of money in and money out. Sit down with someone in the organization's finance department and have that individual walk you through the balance sheet. If you work for a publicly traded company, listen to the quarterly earnings calls.

d. Always know what you want and how to ask for it, e.g., raise, promotion, new or different assignments. At the end of any interview, never forget to say, "I want this job." Be prepared to answer why.

e. Know the value of your skills on the open market. Research online tools, share information with similarly situated friends. Get comfortable asking similarly situated people how much they make and be willing to share how much you make. If solid numbers are just too much for you to ask for, try ranges. The point is, get reliable data. Share information. Rid yourself of the notion that how much you earn is not a statement of you the person. If you are underpaid or under employed, that is only a statement of your need to hone your negotiation skills or a signal for you to upgrade your skills.

f. Negotiate everything. I read the following: "The failure to negotiate for an additional $5,000 at age 22 will cost a woman $500,000 in total lost wages by age 62." As Clark

Howard would say–THAT'S A LOT OF MONEY! Never leave any money on the table. And when I say everything, I mean everything–start times, deadlines, performance goals, severance packages, etc. One additional note here: When asking for a raise, your rising cost of living should be of no consequence to your employer. The focus point has to be is your employer appropriately valuing what you bring to the table? Same is true when you are looking for a job. If you can't put it on a resume, don't say it out loud. For example, "I'm a single mom" is no reason for a potential employer to pay you more than what the job you are applying for is worth.

g. Ask for and respond to feedback. Related to that, never ask a question to which there is only one right answer. It's a set-up for the other person, and it's bad for you in that your behavior will make it difficult for other people to be transparent with you. Take a second to answer this question: When was the last time you asked someone for feedback? In my experience, people who ask for feedback on a monthly basis are the first considered for promotion opportunities and career-enhancing opportunities. People who ask for feedback on a monthly basis and act on it are most likely to succeed when they receive the promotion or the career-enhancing opportunity.

h. Mentor and be mentored. And I don't mean find a buddy with whom you commiserate on a regular basis. Here is a short list of what a mentor or mentors can do for you:

   i. Communicator: They can promote your skills and abilities.

   ii. Long-Term Career Adviser: They can provide input when you are planning for the long term.

iii. Short-Term Career Adviser: They can help you evaluate an offer.

iv. Role Model: Symbolic or actual

v. Sounding Board: Role-play upcoming events like a presentation or a speech

vi. Interpreter: Explain performance feedback you may receive and its implications.

vii. Network: Extending their own network to you or helping you to develop your own network. And you HAVE to mentor. It's one of the ways to answer The Reverend Dr. Martin Luther King, Jr.'s question: "Life's most persistent and urgent question is, 'What are you doing for others?'"

i. Make good decisions and own them no matter the consequences. Sounds simple enough, however, it is difficult to do. Suppose your employer asks you to move. Pro and con the opportunity both in the short- and long-term, as well as the potential impact to you personally and professionally. Ask as many clarifying questions as come to mind. If it works in your favor, great. You own it. If it doesn't pan out, too bad. You still own it. I call making and living with your decisions being a grown-up. BOTTOM LINE: Put your big-girl panties on.

j. You can leave when things are good. You don't have to wait for things at work to go horribly wrong. Leaving for a new experience or a better opportunity is perfectly okay.

Well, that's it. Those are the big ones. One last thing I'd like to share is an old Irish Blessing a mentor once shared with me:

May the road rise up to meet you.
May the wind always be at your back.
May the sun shine warm upon your face,
and rains fall soft upon your fields.
And until we meet again, May God hold
you in the palm of His hand.
All the best to you!

PARTICIPANT 6

As you begin the next chapter of your life, I would suggest that you keep in mind the following guiding principles.

1. Faith: Your foundation for the future will require you to keep your faith. You will have many tests along the way. This is so you can give a 'testimony.' Therefore, you must know that through every challenge, setback, and obstacle, you have not lost or failed. You have gained another opportunity to make a negative a positive. You should look to grow from every door that closes or is broken along the way. You can and will overcome knowing your priorities. Faith is your fundamental basic to success.

2. Do what you are passionate about! Your job should NOT be work, but instead a way to get paid for what you love. Therefore, it is not an issue to get up and go to work. Although no one loves 100% of what they have to do on any job, you should love at least 80% so your strengths are being utilized. You should not be in an environment where you feel that you need to be "fixed" or "changed" to be successful. If that is the case, then you probably are not in the best position for you.

Not to mention that you are not utilizing your strengths, but constantly focusing on "perceived opportunities."

3. Hard work is only a piece of the pie. You must ALWAYS do your best work and try to resolve any issue presented to you, however, the hard work is just the beginning. It is what is expected, but more is required. You are required to do more and to be more than your counterparts. The world is not "fair" and balanced, so you must remove all excuses. Make sure that you continue to invest in yourself through gaining knowledge, i.e. training, workshops, mentoring, special projects, etc. If you don't invest in your future and yourself, how can you ask anyone else to do so? Even though you know this is the case, DO NOT USE IT AS AN EXCUSE!!!! Instead, take those excuses and fuel them into "positive energy of success!" You CAN'T change the world by yourself!

4. Mentors: As you begin your career, you should find mentors and champions. EVERYONE needs a champion to help them maneuver and work through their career. A champion can come through mentoring and/or a working relationship. You should find mentors of different races and genders. Know the strengths and positive characteristics that you want help with from your mentors. You should also develop relationships with colleagues/industry associates/ membership associations. This will develop your network and "self-valuation." Your "valuation" to your discipline and area will come from your knowledge and the respect others have for you. This is built from the network, which you have established.

5. Balance: It is extremely important that you define balance for yourself. What is important to others may not be the

same priority for you in your life. Know that if you get married or have children, your values and requirements will change. As they need you differently at different points of their development, you will change what is important to you along the way. In addition, balance can be achieved by quality and not quantity. The type of relationship that you have with who is important to you and ONLY YOU CAN DEFINE!!!! Each person's sacrifices MUST be decided by each individual. NO ONE can tell you what is RIGHT for you, they can only give you advice and guidance.

I hope that the above 5 guidelines will help you as you hit the world of ADULTHOOD and WORKING.

2

APPRECIATING A FIRM FOUNDATION

THERE ARE UNDOUBTEDLY SOME EXECUTIVES WHO CHARTED THEIR path to the boardroom while still a young person, envisioning their leadership role in a corporation even before finishing high school. Ask them how they climbed the ladder to reach their position of power and the answer may well reveal a professional blueprint sketched while they were still in college, with strategic steps followed to reach every goal as scheduled by a given age—from securing a specific internship before graduation to identifying the company targeted for an entry-level job.

I'm not that person.

While it is true that I developed an unshakable determination and tireless drive during my early days growing up in Kansas City, Missouri, I did not contemplate from my childhood bedroom how I would someday sit at a desk in a company's C-Suite. Nor did I chart out the path I would take to end up in such an executive position. There was no research done regarding the leadership roles I wanted to fill within Corporate America, and I did not have a short list of companies that were my preferred employers.

I never doubted I would continue my education well beyond high school and felt certain I would embark on a successful career, but my earliest professional expectation was that I would rise to lead in the legal realm as an attorney. That was my initial plan as a teenager about to earn my diploma. Not once as a young Black girl did I anticipate that I would excel as an Human Resources executive recognized for my professional expertise in realms ranging from the fundamental talent searches and onboarding duties to developing Diversity, Equity, and Inclusion (DEI) plans, managing communications strategies and media affairs, as well as initiating programs designed to enrich employee opportunities. The roles I have filled as a visionary for specific organizations,

---

Here's a quick summation of my overall expertise and skill set:

- Twenty-plus years of professional experience developing, implementing, and leading strategic Human Resources and People initiatives, plans and practices for broadcast, media, professional services, payroll, customer service, retail management, and global operations.
- Skilled in all areas of Human Capital Management with emphasis on organizational effectiveness, acquisitions and due diligence, employee relations management, diversity management, change management, talent acquisition, executive compensation, benefits and wellness, strategic planning, performance management, leadership development, succession planning and training.

becoming a national voice for change in Corporate America, stepping up as a community leader in a large metropolitan region, and serving as a source of inspiration for aspiring Black women were not part of a master plan devised in my youth.

While my career path and professional achievements were not journaled as a young girl's aspirations or devised years before I took my first job in the business world, they likewise cannot be categorized as the result of happenstance or exceptionally good luck. Endless work, continual perseverance, dogged determination, a commitment to grow through setbacks, and the personal conviction that failure is not an option formed the foundation that I built on throughout my earliest years and yet today. Those building blocks were put in place by my family, primarily my parents DeRay and Fay Cole, who have always been the inspiration for me to go further than I ever dreamed. My maternal grandmother, Luella Kelly, was equally significant in shaping the person I have become. She served as both an anchor and guiding light as I matured from the curious child to the corporate leader situated in the C-Suite.

Family is undoubtedly the most powerful force every individual encounters during their formative years. I specifically recognize my parents and grandmother because they created for me a legacy that is truly unique and exceptional. As previously mentioned, I am a third-generation college graduate. This is unheard of for a Black family, as colleges and universities across the country are still working diligently to entice and enroll primarily first-generation Black students. There are numerous explanations given for why it is that Blacks are underrepresented within higher education enrollments at American institutions, including financial barriers and inferior secondary education opportunities. The fact that such obstacles are still in place makes it even more emotional and meaningful to me when I reflect on the fact that my grandmother received a bachelor's degree in early childhood education and was a kindergarten teacher in her community decades ago when the hurdles were even higher. She had the internal fortitude to go against the cultural norm for a Black female of her age, complete a degree, and consequently set herself apart from her peers.

My parents were equally committed to pursuing a college education. Both continued their studies after finishing their undergraduate experience, each earning a graduate degree. My father earned a bachelor's degree in math and completed a master's degree in biology. He worked as an educator and then a plant manager for years in the field of manufacturing. My grandmother, father, and mother all graduated from the University of Arkansas in Pine Bluff, which is where my mother earned a bachelor's degree in English. I remember during my childhood watching her study to complete a master's degree in library science from Central Missouri State and begin working as a school librarian. My family definitely modeled that you get your degree, and then you get out there in the working world. Once there, you do your absolute best with no excuses and no tolerance for anything less than 100 percent effort 100 percent of the time.

Given such a home dynamic, I gained the mindset as a child that failure was not an option. That conviction impacted all of my endeavors, from studying for the next chapter test in middle school to presenting the end-of-semester project in a high school class. My parents were supportive, and I was determined I would not disappoint them, so I set my standards high and challenged myself to do far more than complete the basic curriculum. Looking back, I would describe myself as the class nerd while attending Ruskin High School in Grandview Missouri, which is a bedroom community just outside of Kansas City.

My high school nickname was "Olive Oil" in reference to the character in the cartoon *Popeye* because I was deemed unattractive by classmates. I was the brainy kid who was a member of student government and a peer counselor. I joined the debate team and thrived on the competition, doing so well that I lettered. The whole experience of researching a topic, developing an argument, preparing for the rebuttal, and then matching wits with a peer taking the opposite stance was invigorating and empowering. I gained self-confidence and built strong public speaking skills. There is no doubt in my mind that the opportunity fueled my desire to be an attorney. I had high hopes and a good dose of optimism as I set my sights on life as a lawyer.

That was all before my life shifted abruptly after I completed my junior year in high school. It was then my father decided and announced that the family would be moving to Atlanta, Georgia. We relocated in order for him to pursue a career advancement opportunity as a turnkey plant manager for a major homebuilding company. The professional door that opened for him created an earthquake in my world. I was anticipating a year of celebration as a senior with friends I had known since my kindergarten days. My plan was to finish strong in the activities I excelled at with a supportive team of teachers I respected and admired. Instead of that scenario, I began my last year of high school feeling like the insecure, incoming freshman student who knew nobody and had to work to find the right locker.

That 800-mile move was without question an extremely difficult transition and as a result, I experienced a rough end to my high school years. I had been an honors student whose experience was absolutely amazing. I would not change one aspect of the three years during which I learned and thrived at Ruskin High School. I felt very safe and secure in Kansas City, where I never had to think about race. Compare that to the school I joined in Georgia, where I was reminded every day that I was a young Black girl. There was so much emphasis put on my gender and race that I struggled to find my place. To this day I marvel that I was the first Black student to speak at graduation. I broke that barrier when I addressed my fellow students at our high school commencement ceremony in 1988.

The move from Missouri to Georgia and all of the struggles I faced as a result of my family relocating to such a different cultural environment when I was still a teenager shaped who I became as an adult. The desire to continue debating disappeared, as did my dream of becoming a lawyer. There was a definite void as I missed what had become an important aspect of my academic experience that had also strengthened me in so many ways as an aspiring student and maturing young lady. I felt I had no option but to make a significant pivot and in doing so, I began to comprehend the concept of resilience as a survival mechanism.

Because of the unexpected move and the need to reinvent myself, I became more jaded and viewed situations with a hint of cynicism. I had always envisioned individuals as being supportive and eager to help each other. That naivete disappeared as I acclimated to Georgia and as a result, I became much more protective of myself and closed off to others. I also developed the mindset of a free agent, which I embrace to this day. I use the term to mean that I became determined to always pursue the best opportunity that surfaces at the best time for me, not allowing the perceptions or expectations of others to limit or control my decisions and actions. This mindset became a mantra that empowered me to question others instead of devaluing myself during tough times when I felt my abilities and worth were being challenged. I consequently became very resilient and very agile as I realized the need to build my self-esteem and self-confidence by always looking inward. I remain grateful that I gained this life skill at an early age, knowing that the move out of my comfort zone in Kansas City created the opportunity to acquire such invaluable wisdom that has guided me through every personal and professional experience.

I packed my free-agent perspective along with what personal items I deemed essential for my residence hall room when it came time to start my undergraduate degree. My spirits were high as I was eager to close the high school chapter and follow in the footsteps of family members as I walked onto a collegiate campus. I arrived at the University of Georgia in Athens (UGA) feeling energized to be part of such a historic institution. UGA was founded in 1785 by a charter that established the school as the first state university in the nation. The first Black students were not enrolled until 1961—more than a century later and just 27 years before I was admitted. These facts are relevant because they reinforce why I felt proud to be a University of Georgia Bulldog. I was carrying on the family legacy at a university with significant history in the state and country.

I started the first semester of my freshman year studying journalism but soon realized I was not going to succeed in that major. I recall feeling very lost and alone as I questioned what field I would pursue. The Department of Family and Consumer Sciences is where I finally felt included and welcomed into the community of students. I began working at the on-campus conference center, which is when I found my passion in the service and hospitality industry. Earning my undergraduate degree in hotel/restaurant management became my goal. An internship completed at the Hyatt Regency in Atlanta sealed my interest in the field. The hiring manager at the premier hotel was amazing, as he took me under his wing as a mentee and taught me the business of hotel service.

And yet, I must confess in all candor that academic excellence was not my top priority during the four years I attended UGA. While I did not abandon the zeal and conviction to do well that were instilled in me during my upbringing, I also found that freedom from living at home brought an unexpected distraction: Guys. I left high school as a student who graduated with honors and somewhat surprisingly, I became a college freshman who focused more on the guys than the grades. There was one particular young man who I connected with and cared about during my entire time as an undergraduate. Hours spent socializing instead of studying were reflected in my final grade point average. I was disappointed in myself for finishing my degree with a transcript that revealed an academic record below what I knew I could have achieved.

My lackluster performance instilled in me the desire to eventually pursue a graduate degree and prove myself as a more stellar student, but my immediate goal was to secure my first full-time professional position. The drive I failed to demonstrate in my coursework at UGA returned as I hustled to find my first employer as a college graduate. The Hyatt Regency internship opened doors immediately and throughout my career because of opportunities that arose through people I met, impressing upon me the importance of creating a professional network and never burning bridges. For example, the hotel manager who had become my mentor reached out to me after years had passed with an offer to come and work alongside him at a major professional services organization.

With no solid career plan in place upon graduation, I cast a wide net during my search for my first job as my time at UGA came to an end. I decided to take a position with Taco Bell, which was a division of PepsiCo Inc. I joined the team at headquarters not many years after PepsiCo had invested approximately $125 million to purchase more than 800 Taco Bell restaurants, elevating them from being known at the regional and state level to status as a national food chain. It was exciting to join such a large corporation, especially given I was assigned to complete a management training program.

One of the most enticing aspects of the position was the rotational format that guaranteed exposure to the various responsibilities of a Human Resources professional. I gathered information and insights into the breadth and importance of such work within any organization. The enormous amount of knowledge I gained about the field piqued my interest, and I decided to pursue an HR career path. The tasks tied to recruiting were especially intriguing, and I found that work particularly enjoyable. This is almost comical to me now as I must confess that after all the years I've completed in Human Resources, I now dread with a passion the prolonged process of completing talent searches!

While I am grateful for the positive aspects of that first job, there unfortunately were also plenty of negative moments as well. The majority were directly tied to my team leader, a female who was dreadful and seemed determined to tear me down. I recognized my lack of experience and took the job expecting constructive criticism that would help me develop in the field. What I experienced instead were blatant attacks and negative assessments about my level of productivity, quality of work, and overall potential. She declared that I was lazy and was quick to make certain I understood that she knew I was not going to reach any level of success if I continued in Human Resources. I certainly was never going to be a leader according to her evaluation of my abilities.

There was no escaping this situation because she oversaw a portion of the program that I had to complete before advancing to the next level of the rotation, which was necessary to finish the training. I could not understand her motivation to be consistently condescending and demeaning. In an attempt to improve our relationship and because I felt a sense of obligation, I accepted an invitation to an event at her home and found her to be much more friendly in that setting. The next day, however, she resumed her belittling behavior.

It did not take long for me to realize that I could not improve or change the work environment I was immersed in at Taco Bell. It was also quickly and abundantly clear that I was not capable of altering my supervisor's behavior toward me or her opinion of my character, abilities, and potential no matter how hard I worked and how well I performed. I felt as if I was in a relationship with an abusive partner. Unable and unwilling to tolerate her continual and blatant hostility, I made the decision after two years to quit. What a happy day it was when I walked away from that toxic environment and took another step forward by returning to the halls of academia. It was 1994 when I once again became a college student, this time at Clark Atlanta University where I enrolled to complete a master's degree in business administration (MBA).

My graduate school experience was markedly different from my undergraduate years for various reasons. The most significant was the fact that I enrolled with a determination to improve my grade point average as one way to counter the lackluster effort I put into earning my bachelor's degree. I also had a clearer vision of my purpose, as I was there to prepare myself for a career in Human Resources. My passion for that work was made clear while working at Taco Bell, despite the difficult circumstances created by my supervisor. Clark Atlanta University did not have an organizational behavior sequence, so I charted out all of my coursework under the umbrella of the MBA to fit with my professional plan.

I felt energized during the two years I committed to being a full-time student at Clark, in part because the university provided a different atmosphere and campus culture than what I experienced at the University of Georgia. This time I not only enrolled in a Historically Black College or University, I joined the first HBCU established in the Southern United States. My parents had attended an HBCU and shared so many memorable moments that I developed and held on to the desire for a similar collegiate experience. I once again was continuing the family legacy and joining the ranks of those who made history at Clark Atlanta University, which was established in 1988 through the consolidation of Atlanta University and Clark College.

Both schools had a rich history, as Atlanta University was founded by the American Missionary Association in 1865. It was the first higher education institution in the country to award graduate degrees to Black students. Clark College has had an equally significant role in the education of Black students. Established in 1869, it became the first liberal arts college offering a four-year degree to a primarily Black student body. Clark Atlanta University remains true to the roots of both parent institutions as it continues to predominantly enroll Black students. The university is a private school still affiliated with the Methodist Church and consequently has a much smaller enrollment than UGA.

All of the unique aspects of Clark Atlanta University resulted in a totally different educational experience for me. I entered an amazing season of growth accelerated by nurturing and encouragement. I went through the MBA program with a cohort of just 64 other students, which created the opportunity to engage with my peers and professors in a meaningful way far beyond chatting while attending lectures together or briefly catching up when connecting outside class to complete capstone projects. There are faculty from that program and fellow graduates who I keep in my circle of friends and professional network still today.

One of the most rewarding aspects of the program was the opportunity to complete an internship with United Technology in Connecticut. I was amazed to realize how the staff welcomed me and expressed a level of excitement about what I could bring to the established team. It was equally surprising to be given a meaningful project. My assignment involved putting together resources the staff needed for DEI programming. That summer I interviewed employees, conducted focus groups, and researched best practices in other organizations.

The culmination of the project was to provide recommendations of my findings, which I presented to the company's leadership team. Focusing on DEI issues proved to be both enlightening and challenging. I felt my confidence and energy levels grow simultaneously as I was steeped in work that was more relevant to the rest of my career than I realized at the time. Of equal importance was the fact that I once again was able to expand my professional network as I gained the respect of staff and supervisors, some of whom not only helped me maximize the internship program but remained essential mentors and advisors to me throughout my career.

By the time I graduated with my MBA in 1996, I was feeling ready to tackle the next level of responsibility in the HR world. Armed with additional knowledge gained along with my graduate degree credential, I felt certain I was destined to take my place in Corporate America and begin my ascent. I felt prepared for and passionate about the opportunities and challenges that were waiting for me further down my professional path. What I did not have was the expectation that each position going forward would present similar challenges to what I had already experienced in my brief tenure at Taco Bell. I was about to enter a working world where I would consistently feel attacked, belittled, dismissed, and ultimately discouraged. Thankfully, the firm foundation that was established by my family and reinforced as I continued to learn at my first job and in the MBA graduate program equipped me to survive the unexpected.

LESSONS LEARNED

Reflection is a powerful tool that I consistently use as a way to assess my progress, reaffirm my strengths, and evaluate ways in which I can improve some aspect of my life or work. When I ponder my earlier years as a young person completing my basic education through the secondary level, I realize that I was richly blessed by family members who established a strong legacy of learning and an equally solid work ethic. They instilled in me a drive and determination that has carried me through every high and low experienced in all stages of my life. If you have had a similar background, rejoice and appreciate what has been instilled in you by those who have guided and loved you, investing in ways that will pay intangible riches. For those who have struggled to find a bedrock or firm foundation on which to build, do not let that reality be an excuse or an obstacle. Find some family member, friend, peer, coworker, supervisor, teacher, or preacher to pour into you the wisdom and guidance you need to execute today while planning for tomorrow.

I also learned at an early age that leaving your comfort zone—or in my case, being pulled away from it by a moving van—can be one of the most effective ways to learn your inner strengths. Just as it takes fire to refine gold, there is a benefit to being tested by new experiences in a different environment that requires rethinking who you are, what you want, and where you are headed. While I can attest from my own experience that these seasons of change are definitely not easy—especially when they do not align with an immediate desire—the end results can be life-changing. In my case, leaving the family home in Kansas City and moving to Atlanta before I had finished high school allowed me to gain valuable insight. I adopted a new perspective as I began to view myself as a free agent empowered to make choices and decisions that were best for me regardless of whatever situation I found myself in at a given moment. I encourage you to build your own philosophical lens and use it to counter the naysayers or dissect situations where you feel crippled and unable to reach your potential.

Perhaps the most important bit of wisdom I gleaned from this stage of my life was that there are times when quitting is not a sign of failure, surrender, or incompetence. Because of my free agent mindset, I was able to leave a toxic job where I was not only stifled but intentionally deflated. I found the strength and peace to realize I was not failing but rather was stuck in a situation where I could not grow so I had to go. I chose to embody and demonstrate what it means to be a free agent. I made the move forward in a different direction by completing my master's degree in business administration. I caution you to evaluate every situation before making such a bold move but when you have done the assessment, if it becomes apparent that there is no way for you to bring positive change or find a way to grow rather than be pushed down, then the time is right to get out. It is OK to say *"I quit!"* This is what I mean when I encourage Black women to find their voice and be courageous in using it. Speak your truth and move forward.

3

SEARCHING FOR FERTILE GROUND

FAITH WAS ANOTHER IMPORTANT CORNERSTONE OF MY EARLY YEARS. With church attendance a family priority, I realized long before adulthood what it means to honor God and make Him the center of my life. Since my days of attending Sunday School as a child, I have been captivated and intrigued by the parables from the Bible. These simple stories that Christ added to His teachings in the New Testament illustrate a spiritual truth in such a way that it is easy to understand, remember, and apply to daily life. One that has always stayed with me is from the book of Matthew and describes the results of a farmer sowing seed that scatters so that it lands across a path, among rocks, within weeds, and on dirt. Only the seeds that fall into the rich soil take root and produce a crop.

With my MBA completed, I felt much like the farmer in the parable. I was ready to plant professional seeds and reap a bountiful career. I quickly learned, however, how hard it is as a Black female to find fertile ground in Corporate America where the nurturing necessary to grow is available. I also had plenty of weeds begin to crop up in both my professional and personal life during the years immediately following graduation in 1996.

I married my first husband that same year. We met through one of my mentors in the MBA program and dated during the time I was steeped in academic work as a full-time student. He proposed just as I was completing the coursework for my degree. I surprised myself by saying yes, as I never thought I would marry. Frankly, I never anticipated anyone would propose to me because I still had recollections of myself as that nerdy high school girl once referred to as "Olive Oil." I never daydreamed about the moment when someone would pledge their love to me and ask me for a lifetime commitment because I did not define myself as that girl who became a bride.

I am confident that my family history once again influenced my decision to accept the proposal, as my grandparents were married in 1941 when they were 23 and 24 years old, respectively. They were a couple for 63 years until my grandmother passed away. My parents have had an equally exceptional relationship, as they have celebrated 55 years together as a married couple. It is consequently not surprising that part of me became convinced finding a spouse should be among my accomplishments. By marrying, I was continuing yet another strong legacy.

Taking on the new role as wife did not diminish my desire to acquire a leadership position in Corporate America. I was still determined and eager to work in the field of Human Resources, a quest that I reignited by taking a job with Pizza Hut. The chain was under the PepsiCo Inc. division, so I was returning to the same parent company as my Taco Bell days. I am forever grateful for the opportunity to start building the foundation of my career at Pepsi, which is the company where I obtained my first HR job and experienced my initial professional growth spurts. My employment started in the spring of 1997, approximately the same time Pizza Hut was becoming increasingly daring and creative with marketing messages. For example, professional American boxer Muhammad Ali appeared in one commercial that year, and another advertising spot with former Soviet Union President Mikhail Gorbachev was in production for release the following year.

It was consequently an interesting time to join the company as a regional Human Resources manager/leader who was assigned to work as an HR Generalist. I managed two staff professionals and was given oversight of all employee relations issues for more than 63 restaurants in my assigned geographical area across three states. Some of the restaurants were franchised and others were owned by the company. My work involved ensuring there was adequate staffing at each site and that each team member had been trained. The responsibilities were broad and the task list lengthy. I grasped the fundamentals of how to be an HR professional, which led to an understanding of the foundational work tied to the field. For example, I learned how to recruit, train, improve employee relations, and manage and lead a staff. Such knowledge was integral to my growth and development as an HR executive.

I welcomed the wide range of assignments in my first significant role in the field. While there was definitely a learning curve, I found myself blessed and enriched by some intelligent, caring, and driven colleagues. Rodney Whitmore was one gentleman I

The following is a summation of my duties and some key accomplishments while working in the role as an HR Manager.

- Responsible for launching tactical activities on staffing, payroll, training, new hire orientation, employee relations, employee programs and special events, employee file audits and managing federal and local legal compliance requirements
- Decreased turnover by 14 percent
- Teamed with line clients and other functional groups to achieve profitability goals
- Proactively improved employee relations through an employee concern resolution process that included arbitration
- Led culture change toward positive recognition and front line focus
- Developed and managed restaurant management recruiting plans
- Monitored all staffing levels and developed plans for addressing critically understaffed facilities
- Executed Human Resource succession and development plans for all employees
- Responded to and managed outside interventions including EEOC, union activities, and Department of Labor inquiries
- Conducted training seminars for retention, labor awareness, leadership effectiveness, and career development

met while he was serving as HR Regional Director. He graciously welcomed me to the Pizza Hut management team and was always ready to provide objective and direct feedback. Rodney quickly became an amazing mentor and leader who taught me the importance of knowing your profession, using data to tell the story, and creating lasting and meaningful relationships. I respected his knowledge then and still value it today as he remains in my network as a mentor, sponsor, and close friend.

While I was blessed and nurtured by the time I spent working with Rodney at Pizza Hut, there were unfortunately others in the office who made the daily environment unpleasant if not difficult. One was the lady who became my boss when Rodney transitioned to an elevated role in another organization. She was younger than me and for whatever reason, chose a behavior that made our interactions strained. Beyond engaging in combative behavior and consistently being incredibly condescending, she micro-managed, was difficult to follow, and took credit for the body of work that others on the team accomplished.

While I have no doubt that I could have certainly survived in the Pizza Hut HR office and definitely was capable of completing the responsibilities of my position that I held for nearly three years, I was not being nurtured and saw no path for advancement. I therefore once again made the decision to leave my job. I do not want to minimize the potential stress and emotional toll that comes with rendering your resignation and walking away from secure employment. There are multiple reasons worry will creep in and complicate making the decision to pursue such a potentially drastic professional change that definitely impacts your personal world as well.

In my case, the fact that I had given birth to my first child certainly was one reason to consider staying put, given I was in a stable situation doing work that I enjoyed. The added load of caring for an infant son would undoubtedly complicate taking a new position. But remember that I view life through my free-agent lens, and I was certain I was ready to seize the next opportunity. It is important to note that I planned my departure in such a way that I left on good terms with my superiors and staff. I had already discovered in my relatively short career the power of building and protecting a positive professional network. Just how important such a connection is with individuals from past employment situations was made apparent when I accepted my next job offer.

I began in my new position in 2000 as People Capability Manager for an online supermarket business on the recommendation of a gentleman who had heard of my work from during the time we were both employed at Taco Bell. I did not partner with him directly on any projects, as he was on the company's international side of operations. That fact makes his efforts to have me join the team of the online business headquartered out of Seattle, Washington, so much more remarkable. It also became an important reminder that while I can be convinced my efforts are unnoticed as I toil away at my work, I may in fact be capturing the attention of someone within the organization. I was completely unaware of the ways in which I was making a positive impression across divisions while at Taco Bell for such a short time.

My new employer's goal was to radically shift the traditional grocery shopping paradigm by offering fresh seafood, meat, and produce online at prices comparable to what could be found at the neighborhood store. The company developed its own technology to support the online orders and handle the routing of delivery trucks from centers that were scattered across the country and stayed open seven days a week. At its peak, the company had sales that topped $1.5 million per day, making it the largest and most successful internet grocery business in existence at that time. My oversight as the People Capability Manager was again broad in scope, with responsibilities for all HR tasks ranging from recruiting to staffing, hiring, training, development initiatives, and employee engagement. Other duties involved ensuring safety standards were in place and followed, as well as playing a lead role in the functioning of the company's Customer Fulfillment Center. It was an exciting opportunity to expand my knowledge and gain experience in an entirely different operation, as there were not many companies in the year 2000 as tech-savvy or confidently bold in using the

Internet for an entire business model's foundation. I embraced the opportunity to reveal what type of leader I could be and showcase my management skills.

As the manager in this position, I was responsible for the opening of the Customer Fulfillment Center and creating the HR back office that would be used in the facility. I hired site staff to include as my direct report. We became a scrappy and ingenious HR team of two. One of the most valuable lessons learned while in this position was the importance of how to pivot. During this time, the company was preparing to open a facility. The critical milestones had been met as the leadership team was in place, staff had been hired, and the stock was available so that orders could begin to be processed and filled. One week before the actual launch date, the company was acquired and shut down. It was incredibly disappointing that we did not get to open the center

---

The following is a summation of my duties while working as a People Capability Manager:

- Responsible for leading the HR function by overseeing the conceptualization and management of all HR projects for the Southeast locations
- Responsible for leading all people-related activities tied to a Customer Fulfillment Center (CFC)
- Ensured that all positioned within the CFC were staffed in a cost-effective manner with high-quality talent that represented a diverse workforce
- Ensured that all associates were well trained; calibrated training and sought opportunities for improvement
- Ensured internal equity in salary and bonus administration
- Provided confidential counsel to the director of the Customer Center General Manager to help ensure his/her success.
- Ensured that all safety standards were being adhered to and a safety program existed
- Maintained all associates' records for the facility and ensured that the human resource information system (HRIS) database was accurate

---

after all the work the team put in to make it the best facility in the Southeast.

I am confident there was much more knowledge I could have accumulated and contributions I would have made while working in this position, but instead I gained a completely different experience when the company was sold. I was suddenly and unexpectedly without a job after just eight months. The pink slip arrived when I was seven months pregnant with my second child, another son. That was in the fall of 2000, another season in my life when resilience became crucial as I was unemployed and overwhelmed.

There is an extra amount of confidence and energy required when being thrust into an unplanned job search while very pregnant and caring for a toddler. My inherent belief that failure is not an option motivated me to hustle for my next position, which I found within weeks of losing my job, despite the fact I was nine months pregnant when I interviewed on a Friday. I honestly did not have time to mentally dissect how well the conversations had gone because I gave birth the next day. A couple days later I received a call for a second interview, which I was able to postpone long enough that I could shop for something that would fit given my closet was filled with maternity clothes. Just two days after the second interaction, I was offered an HR manager's position. The fact they agreed to an eight-week delay for my start date given I had a newborn made me confident I was joining an excellent company where I could further pursue my career.

I could not begin to fathom the opportunities that awaited me with the corporation I was joining, which had a national reach and expertise in helping companies find solutions for managing HR functions. I was enthusiastic to have reached a new level of involvement in Corporate America by working for a company with such a broad vision and scope, and consequently stayed with the firm from 2000 to 2006. Walking into my office that first day, I was feeling beyond excited and closer to euphoric as I contemplated the possibilities.

The luster unfortunately soon faded as I dealt with a belligerent recruiter who I supervised. I had obviously managed employees with varying personalities in my other positions, but no previous individuals under my leadership so blatantly refused to comply and be a team player. She rejected any direction from me and ignored my feedback. As I was trying to understand the leadership team that I was a member of, she consistently went to my peers and boss about the disdain she felt working for me. Her behavior continued to be undermining and manipulative.

Once again, I found myself in a strained work environment made even more intolerable by the fact I learned my rebellious direct report earned a paycheck that exceeded mine. I always had access to salary information given my HR responsibilities, so it was not difficult to compare my level of compensation relative to others in the organization. This was my first experience with salary inequity and a salary compression, which cemented my desire to advance in my career. I was still not certain exactly what that would entail or where I would ultimately land, but I recommitted to focusing on my work and not the office drama around me that I determined was noise I needed to tune out. The fact I was the major breadwinner in the household that now included two young children further fueled my ambition.

I was consequently thrilled to be promoted to a director's position shortly after being hired, and not merely because of the salary increase. This new title reflected a rise in status, as I had remained a manager in all of my previous positions. With the elevated title came more authority and responsibility, which I embraced as an invigorating challenge. My role as HR Director was to provide oversight for strategic planning, leadership development, talent management, organizational development, product and leadership training, and HR transactions for all of the company's U.S. locations. I also developed and managed the associates who provided professional support in the areas of benefits, employee relations, recruitment, training, payroll, and performance management.

I was delighted to focus on my role as an Human Resource leader with assigned clients and even more enthused by the fact I was a strategic thought partner with the leaders I supported. I focused on building a team of HR professionals to help me drive the initiatives that were imperative to impact leadership effectiveness and team development, as well as provide support and guidance to teams that were integral to the overall growth of the organization. As opposed to other jobs I held that were heavily transactional with direction decided and provided outside the HR unit, this was the first role that I was part of the people strategy with the leaders in their respective functions or business lines.

One goal that I bring into every new position is to continue expanding my professional network by adding mentors, advisors, and friends. During my time with this firm, I was blessed to develop such a professional relationship with the gentleman who at the time was serving as the president of the corporation's benefit services. He was an executive who began teaching me the valuable lesson of using your voice. He also showed me what compassion looks like in a leader. I will never forget the phone call that he had with me on a Saturday about my career and subsequent conversations we engaged in when I served as a director in his organization. I would often be in awe because he was the president of the division.

Had it not been for the influence of this colleague, I would have left my job in 2004 when I received an offer to join Aramark. The opportunity to become part of the HR team for the U.S. company that operates in 14 countries delivering food services, facilities management, and uniform services was incredibly enticing. It was also flattering to realize that my work was being noticed to the point that I was receiving unsolicited job opportunities, a reality that bolstered my confidence. When I made it known that I was contemplating my departure, steps were taken to increase both my leadership role and salary.

I took on additional duties as Diversity Director, which I envisioned would prove to be more fertile ground where I would

---

The following is a summation of my duties while working as an HR Director:

- Completed the strategic planning, leadership, talent management, organizational development, product and leadership training and Field HR businesses working across the U.S. locations utilizing direct supervision, matrix management, and business partnerships to execute people leadership initiatives

- Led the training to facilitate all training required for an effective workforce

- Evaluated business needs and set strategic direction for specific client groups and assisted with staffing levels and succession planning and conducted bench-planning sessions with division executive team

- Implemented all diversity initiatives in the region that were adopted in National Account Services

- Provided leadership on special projects in specific HR areas including diversity initiatives, Gallup Q12, and DDI Targeted Selection

- Conducted compensation planning to include bonus, stock plans, and executive compensation plans

- Spearheaded all employee relations and investigations to bring closure to complaints, reduce legal exposure and settle lawsuits, resulting in a 35% decrease in claims filed

---

plant new seed and further expand my skill set and expertise. In this new role, I was responsible for all grassroot efforts in leading diversity recruiting by identifying strategic partners, schools, and professional organizations to build a pipeline for diverse recruiting and hiring. I had to focus on the relationships that I held internally and externally to drive diversity recruiting at a time when it was not considered a priority. I consequently realized anew the importance of networking and creating meaningful relationships, which has followed me throughout my career.

But let's not forget the weeds mentioned in the parable and their ability to choke out growth regardless of how rich the soil. They cropped up shortly after I began the additional duties as Diversity Director in large part because the Chief Human Resources Officer (CHRO) made the decision that I would report to a peer who held a parallel director's position. For the first time in my career, I began to experience microaggressions that were so unexpected I did not initially recognize the behaviors I was experiencing as attacks. Of equal surprise to me was that the negativity I increasingly encountered came from two females, which also opened my eyes to the reality that women in Corporate America are more often combative and attacking than supportive of their female coworkers.

The trouble began when the peer who was functioning as my boss moved me into a cubicle, which was another first, as I had always been assigned to an office in every position I held. While it may seem insignificant, the physical shift from private office space to a desk in an open cubicle signaled to me and others a downgrade. Beyond such actions, there were derogatory words meant to deflate me. We were working on the same project as directors and while doing so, my peer boss bluntly stated that I

The following is a summation of my duties while working as Diversity Director, which is a role I took on while still serving the firm as HR Director:

- Created the diversity strategies and developed the business division initiatives on workplace diversity, workplace diversification plans and change management strategies. Key responsibilities included coaching Executive Committee on minority relations and developing people leadership and designing college's relations programs

- Executed diversity initiatives for National Account Services and Benefit Services to include the Executive Diversity Council and Regional Diversity Councils

- Created the diversity scorecard to measure success by analyzing metrics

- Managed outside relations with diversity organizations, including INROADS, National Black MBA Association, and National Sales Network

- Consulted regions on recruitment and development for women and people color initiatives

- Developed grassroots initiatives for retaining women and people of color into the organization

- Executed organizational development interventions for projects to include succession planning, leadership development and team effectiveness to create a diverse workforce

- Project managed all diversity community involvement

- Completed organizational development interventions for clients to ensure team effectiveness through different strategic approaches, including Gallup Q12

would never have the ability to lead in a corporation because, in her opinion, I was ineffective.

While I do not anticipate building a close bond with every person I partner with in the workplace, I had never experienced such hostility from a colleague. I could not understand why this white woman who was older than me appeared to be threatened by my presence and position in the company. I was equally baffled when years later our paths crossed again at an event where she had the audacity to introduce me as a former colleague who she had identified as a professional with high potential. Perhaps she felt compelled to tell such a lie because I had reached the level of working as a CHRO. I refrained from making the rest of the room aware of the hostility she exhibited that made our relationship contentious during those days I spent in the cubicle. Another blow during the same timeframe occurred when a different white female who was working as a manager on the team I supervised was promoted above me to become a senior director. Her husband had a close relationship with our CHRO and she had more education than I had completed.

As I contemplated what was happening around me and all that was being hurled directly at me, I had a watershed moment that I still consider to be an awakening from my naivete. I came to the painful realization that there are times when some people cannot be trusted. In much the same way the experience at my new high school in Atlanta made me see the reality that individuals do not inherently help each other, I woke up to the harsh truth that Corporate America is filled with as much hostility as hope. I responded by compartmentalizing and internalizing all the negativity I was encountering, which was oddly deflating and simultaneously empowering. I resolved to fight and work even harder as a way to disprove the doubters who surrounded me.

In all candor, I did not see any other option but to stand strong at that time. Remember that my family instilled that failure is not an option. I was left with the choice of either quitting—which in this situation would signal that I had failed— or becoming bitter and an equally impossible employee. Neither is in my character. I also had the added burden of being the major breadwinner for my household that included a spouse who was increasingly resentful of the time I devoted to my career. There were consequently tensions steadily mounting at home as work became increasingly intolerable. The profession still fascinated me and my eagerness to complete the assignments I had been given never waned. I was just struggling to see how I could get through the weeds to reach the goal of doing my work well and advancing in the company.

Without realizing it at the time, I had become one of myriad Black women tangled in the dilemma of how to find position and power in Corporate America. The extent of the struggle became more apparent while I was completing research for my dissertation as part of my doctorate, which I decided to pursue because of what I was experiencing in my professional role. Once again, I was certain that additional education would give me the confidence and credentials I needed to better understand the dysfunctional office dynamics I had endured and, perhaps most importantly, provide an advantage that I could use to unlock professional doors.

LESSONS LEARNED

Growth in a career truly is similar in many ways to how a crop develops. It takes patience, hard work, and a good dose of faith for the farmer to start with a tiny seed and anticipate a bountiful crop. Likewise, I quickly learned that all three elements are vital to finding success in Corporate America. My work at Pizza Hut and in the following two companies made me realize the value of taking incremental steps forward with a focus on growth. I was not obsessed with titles but rather more intent on developing my skills and maturing as both a person and a professional leader. I wanted to be a better version of myself as I improved in my HR roles and duties, which I did in part because of strong mentors who built my confidence and became a source of encouragement.

Once I was hired by a third business in the manager role yet again, I realized my goal was to be a director. I quickly grasped the wisdom in always thinking ahead to the next step, but I never looked too far down the path. I did not begin to contemplate arriving in the C-Suite once I became a director, but I did after a couple years in that role envision myself serving as a vice president. This patient approach has allowed me to be diligent with the task at hand, constantly learning and applying knowledge so that I am ready for the next step. There is far less pressure navigating the career path with such a plan that allows you to be comfortable with a steady pace and maximize the growth potential in each position along the way.

A key aspect to finding success with such a plan is that it requires you do indeed keep moving forward. I realized within just the first five years of my career how important it is to push myself not only with the daily tasks but in how I viewed opportunities. Remember the danger of the comfort zone. I could have easily stayed parked in positions that were adequate but not excellent in terms of my own ambitions and capabilities. It takes effort to be open to change, especially if you are content with your career status. Do not let your current success or satisfaction keep you from contemplating options that move you in a different direction. Have confidence in yourself to know what you need to go forward and seek that out, whether it be in the position you hold or the job you envision. When you are ready for the next step, leave your position on good terms, which means never quit in a rage. A planned departure with time for your employer to handle the vacancy is always your best option because you must protect your reputation as well as your professional network. There is always the possibility that coworkers or supervisors from your past will reappear in a future work situation.

Regardless of the company you select or the position you fill, understand and anticipate that you will encounter negative forces. While there will undoubtedly be difficult assignments that create tense situations, it is more likely that the stress will arise because of individuals who introduce conflict. Microaggressions often experienced by Black women are so deflating that a survival strategy is necessary. I quickly realized that my response was to internalize such attacks, especially early in my career when I did not have the courage to speak out against the behavior. There were many sleepless and emotional nights as I contemplated what was wrong with me and what I needed to change about myself to be and do better.

Looking inward is valuable, as there are always lessons we can learn about ourselves and ways we can improve. In fact, you cannot and will not continue to grow and learn until you are able to complete a self-examination that allows you to understand what you contributed to a situation or exchange. This type of reflection leads to positive change. It is equally important, however, that personal analysis does not become an exercise in berating yourself. Understand and embrace the fact that your response is consequently as significant as the negative event. You will sink deeper into a pit of depression, self-doubt, and inaction until and unless you realize that you cannot completely control or change an environment in which you are attacked. The individuals who are causing the conflict and attempting to deflate you have issues that they must resolve. Most importantly, do not let their shortcomings and negative or aggressive behavior as an employee or person become an indictment of who you are and what you are capable of accomplishing. Do not translate their issues into your sense of failure but rather engage others in addressing the behavior, which I realize once again requires courage of voice.

4

SILENCING THE NAYSAYERS

Anticipation is a powerful force of anxious suspense that we experience throughout life. It exists beginning in our earliest years when as small children we struggle to wait for the opening of a Christmas present and continues to manifest when as young adults we watch for that college acceptance letter to arrive or hope for the phone call that results in a job offer. Whether it be the completion of an academic degree, the start of a career, waking on your wedding day, or welcoming home a newborn, the most memorable moments are always coupled with an excitement and eagerness for what wonderful opportunities and happiness lie ahead.

I felt such energy as I returned to the University of Georgia to complete my doctorate, despite the fact my motivation for enrolling was in part to counter negative experiences that had occurred in the workplace early in my career. Another factor that played into the decision to continue my education was my growing conviction that a master's degree was not enough to catapult me into the leadership roles I desired or put me at the table in boardrooms where I wanted to be seated. I did not, however, anticipate that my experiences in the Ph.D. program would serve as a microcosm of what I would continue to encounter and endure as a Black woman advancing in the HR field.

As I contemplated pursuing yet another degree, I briefly returned to my earlier interest in a career as a lawyer and pondered if a law degree would be the best option. I again relied on my professional network as I explored the possibilities before finalizing a plan. A colleague working as an attorney gave me the insight I needed to decide I would earn the doctorate, which I did knowing with confidence I would not use the credential to serve as a faculty member. Teaching on a campus was never my dream or desire. I was instead going after another key that I felt certain would allow me to open more doors in Corporate America.

Given my family influence and learning legacy, it is not surprising that I turned to education as a solution to the challenges I was facing at the start of my career. My initial jobs in the profession had proven that nothing was going to be given to me, but rather every opportunity had to be earned and every promotion hard fought. I had already been enlightened to the fact that I was going to have to show up better than anybody else and push harder to reach the next rung on the corporate ladder. I had contemplated for quite some time the question of how I could improve myself and was ready to pursue the answer. By completing a doctorate, I was positioning myself to have more education than others in the room and show up ready for the next leadership role I envisioned.

That end goal was the motivation I needed to persist throughout the intense program that was made more exhausting by the fact I continued to work full time and was caring for two children while enduring a tumultuous marriage. I lived approximately 50 miles from the campus, which only lengthened the hours of already long days spent meeting my work and family obligations. The nurturing I had appreciated while earning my MBA and hoped I would find again with my student peers and faculty was not present during my doctoral journey, in part because the program was designed for full-time students. I soon realized that my professors were not impressed by my ability to juggle the graduate classes with such a heavy load at work and home. They instead interpreted my continuing to work as a sign that I was not committed to completing the degree and made the assumption that I would stop progressing on the academic path long before crossing the commencement stage.

That mindset was apparent as I endured both passive and aggressive attacks while I completed the coursework and prepared for the mandatory comprehensive exams. As one example, a faculty member commented on a paper I had written that it was clear I was not able to deal with situations where I was not in control. Another professor bluntly stated his conviction that while I might be able to pass all of the class requirements, I would end up as just another ABD student, meaning all but the dissertation was completed. Still others told me that I was not committed to the program and did not take it seriously because I did not quit my job and solely focus on my doctoral journey as a full-time student.

The perception that I was a lesser student surfaced even more clearly through the interactions I had with the chair of the committee that would decide if I remained in the program and would also shepherd the lengthy dissertation process. She was a white female who held a Ph.D. and had served as a director in HR prior to leaving the corporate world to work in academia. Any hope that our common professional interest would result in a bond quickly faded as she intentionally made my graduate school experience difficult, and not in the sense of academic rigor. I was feeling attacked as she questioned why I would not resign from my position and put all of my efforts into earning the degree. I felt encouraged if not pressured to drop out because it was clear faculty members who I had anticipated would support my academic work and aid in my progress instead were adamant in thinking I was not going to make it to the hooding ceremony.

The harsh words and presumption of failure stung in part because I was one of very few Black females in the program. I could not help but wonder if the faculty provided more support to the other students. I still vividly recall feeling so devastated just one semester prior to sitting for the comprehensive exams that I was in tears for the entire 45-minute commute home, and I am not a crier. The feelings of defeat and thoughts of quitting that were prevalent when I started the car on campus had evolved into an angry determination by the time I pulled into the driveway. I was resolved that I would finish every requirement for the degree, including the dissertation. Each of my committee members had the credential that I wanted, and I would not let the ugly noise being shouted at me divert or defeat me. I'd be damned if I did not become Dr. DeRetta Rhodes.

I was equally committed to making a change in my committee, as I was not going to tolerate the attacks from the unsupportive chair—a professor who should have been my strongest advocate and a source of encouragement—as I headed into the hefty task of conducting research and writing the dissertation. The only strategy I could develop to replace her was to shift from the Doctor of Education (Ed.D.) program in adult education that I had enrolled in initially and instead follow the curriculum for the Doctor of Philosophy (Ph.D.), even though that meant adding more classes and a stronger emphasis on research. I was blessed that a professor who I connected with agreed to join the committee, as she became the inspiring mentor I needed to get to graduation. She spoke truth when she told me that completing the degree would change my life, which at the time was frankly in shambles.

What none of my collegiate peers or faculty knew was that I had another strong motivation for completing the doctorate, a very personal reason tied to the fact that my marriage was crumbling. That private reality also explained why I literally could not afford to enroll in the graduate program as a full-time student. I had to remain employed because I knew a divorce was imminent. I provided the primary income for the family and would soon be solo in supporting my two sons, who were then 8 and 10. I was about to become the stereotype of the single Black mother, but that was much preferred to remaining in the debilitating relationship.

My husband had become yet another negative force in my life. Perhaps that is why the harsh words from faculty hit so hard, as I was already hearing at home from my spouse that I was a failure. He repeatedly stated that I was void of emotion, concerned about nothing other than climbing the corporate ladder and making money, and that I was destined to have a horrible relationship with our sons because of my misplaced priorities. He felt such resentment—and I truly believe jealousy to some extent—that he would predict with pleasure that I was destined to fall hard into loneliness. I particularly remember he would often state that a doctorate was not going to keep me warm at night. My response was that it would pay the bills, which was a burden I carried and was about to become significantly heavier after the divorce in ways I could never have anticipated.

The lack of affection and connection between us was revealed in part by his frequently referring to me as "Ice Princess." What he witnessed was my ability to control my emotions, as I had learned that in some situations it is better that they not be on display. I was actually experiencing plenty of emotional angst as a result of our relationship, which I had come to realize years earlier was a mistake. I should never have married him, as I lacked the trust needed for us to build a healthy and happy home. Instead, a competitive struggle existed between us to the point of toxicity, yet we created a façade that hid the marital woes. For example, we purchased a home that was well beyond our means, draining my 401K to finance the property. We stretched the marriage to 12 years but there was nothing that would save us from divorce, which was finalized in 2008.

Shortly after, I realized that my instinct to withhold trust was an internal warning sign I should have heeded. When we were together, my husband took responsibility for filing the taxes. Within months of the marriage ending, I was contacted by the IRS and made aware of the fact that he had not actually filed for the previous five years. I owed $195,000 in back taxes. All the security I felt working for a Fortune 500 company while holding an MBA degree and completing a doctorate disappeared in an instant as I realized I was a broke single Black lady with two young sons. It became clear that while my ex-husband saw my commitment to my work as a detriment, I and my sons would have been destitute had I not excelled at my job and remained steadfast in my career. Once again my professional network proved invaluable, as a mentor connected me with a tax accountant. He negotiated the debt down to $89,000, which I paid over five years at $800 a month. I downgraded the car and foreclosed on the house, moving into a rental property where I stayed with my children until my parents graciously purchased a home for the three of us.

As much as the family support was a huge blessing, I also felt an additional cloud of despair because there had never been a divorce among my relatives. Marriage was a commitment for eternity, as demonstrated by my parents' union of more than 50 years and counting, as well as my grandparents who remained a couple until my grandmother's passing. It was a struggle to not feel that I had failed because my marriage fell apart. I countered those negative emotions by realizing that I would not have finished my Ph.D. had we stayed together, as he was not supportive. There was some additional level of comfort in realizing that a high percentage of women pursuing a doctorate experience a divorce, but that fact did not make my personal struggle to reach graduation day any easier.

It took me seven years to complete my Ph.D. During that time, my grandmother died, and I went through the divorce. I had to manage an enormous amount of unexpected debt and find a way to provide for my sons, enacting a plan that involved disrupting their lives further as we moved to a new address. I continued a full-time job and added a commute to the campus where I tackled a hefty academic load, including the research required for my dissertation, all while fighting against the doubts faculty openly expressed. I added fortitude to my resilience and as a result, I did indeed cross the commencement stage.

That was a day of sweet celebration in 2010, as my sons witnessed what it means to persist and conquer against all odds.

It was an exceptional moment for me personally because my lead professor on the committee who had been so supportive was traveling in South Africa and unable to present my diploma at the ceremony. One of the professors who told me I would never graduate consequently had to look me in the eye as he placed the regalia around my neck at the hooding. I was ecstatic relishing the fact that I had silenced my nemesis by proving my perseverance.

In addition to all that I experienced personally while completing the doctorate, there was also upheaval in my professional life as I changed jobs three times during the years I was once again a student. The first shift came just two years into my studies, when I decided to leave my position as an HR Director and Diversity Director at the corporation I had joined nearly six years earlier. From the moment I was moved into a cubicle at that organization, I knew my days were numbered even though I had not specifically planned to leave before completing the degree. My discontent was obvious by the fact that I did not unbox what I carried over from my office, which was my public statement that I was not going to tolerate such disrespect and would be departing sooner versus later. The decision to keep my items packed made it much easier to clean out my workspace when another job opportunity surfaced.

A door unexpectedly opened in 2006 and I eagerly walked through it to become a Diversity Director focused on leading inclusiveness and flexibility initiatives. I was the first person hired into the newly created position at the company that was one of the nation's top accounting firms. This company was among the largest privately-owned corporations in the United States with offices and clients around the world. The position came to my attention because the person who had hired me for an internship years earlier called and encouraged me to apply. I am forever thankful that he believed in my abilities and gave me the push needed to change directions yet again, as I would have otherwise missed an opportunity to build a new HR unit in an international firm. I would have missed out on one of the best jobs of my career.

I learned from the leaders in the organization while in this role, specifically a cohort of women who created a sense of awe within me as I observed their poise, talent, and the power of their presence. I was blessed and fortunate to gain insights from each of them. The men that I encountered were equally strong mentors and sponsors for me in my role. I truly believe that iron sharpens iron, which is what I experienced as I not only learned the business but created relationships that I still hold today. I had the opportunity to focus on my professional brand and hone my skills as a leader in a role where I had influence to make an impact.

The following is a summation of my duties while working as an HR Diversity Director/Inclusiveness and Flexibility Leader:

- Responsible for developing programs in the Southeast, Puerto Rico, and Caribbean to create and enhance inclusiveness and workforce flexibility throughout the organization.

Leadership Development duties:

- Responsible for establishing strategic direction for two divisions focusing on building management capability, performance-driven results, and people development processes in collaboration with the Partners and Principals with the Southeast practice
- Contribute to company performance through the development of strategic planning and tactical implementation of people processes and tools to support a global business of 578 professional and executive-level employees throughout the Southeast

Change Management duties:

- Create and implement a workforce flexibility strategy to enhance work-life balance and retention of high-potential women and people of color

---

I am confident that I became a better professional because of the working partnerships that I developed as this firm's Diversity Director. An important person who I met in a previous role became a significant advisor to me and was instrumental in teaching and guiding me as I assumed the responsibility of addressing and enriching inclusiveness across the mega corporation. I learned from my mentor the importance of the body of work of diversity and inclusion. I also had stellar team members who I led with the conviction that we would rise together as we tackled endeavors that were new for the corporation and oftentimes beyond what we had accomplished individually in our previous positions. We specifically worked on a recruitment and engagement strategy that increased the talent of women and people of color in the business unit in which it was implemented.

And yet, I once again faced challenges presented by individuals who were anything but positive. At this company, the struggles developed when another Black female who was clearly not supportive became my supervisor. She micromanaged programs I was involved in prior to her becoming my leader, initiatives that were of such significance they could lift my career and consequently impact my future. She was not aware of the relationships that I had diligently established and was constantly criticizing the work that had already been cemented. In addition to the worsening relationship with my manager, I was quickly becoming aware of the fact that my future with this company was limited. I would not be able to gain partnership in the firm unless I became a certified public accountant, which was not part of my long-term plan, especially given I was still completing the work required to earn the Ph.D.

In addition, my oversight of diversity and inclusiveness initiatives meant that I was increasingly building an expertise in the DEI niche. That was not the career destination I envisioned for myself going forward. I had no desire to become planted in such work, yet I was on track to be pigeon-holed in that realm of HR despite being employed in the role for slightly less than two years. I consequently made another job change while in the midst of finalizing my divorce and finishing my degree. I shifted in 2008 and became part of a media conglomerate's Human Resources team.

Often throughout my career, the opportunity for me to make a professional move has surfaced because of someone from my past. A professional friend, a colleague from a former workplace, or someone who I had crossed paths with while completing a degree became aware of a vacancy and made a phone call to suggest the possibility of an excellent fit. Typically, I directly received the courtesy notice from such an individual but this time, the company reached out to assess my interest in joining the international operation after a gentleman I had met in a class made the Human Resources office aware of my skill set. I was hired as the HR Director supporting the Chief Financial Officer and all of the departments under that unit.

Anticipation was once again my dominant emotion and thankfully, it countered the discouragement I was feeling overall given the graduate school drama and draining divorce process. I was quickly immersed in yet another new realm of Corporate America, applying my HR knowledge to completely different work scenarios and challenges. The work was invigorating and the accomplishments sweet. Creating a high-performance team was my goal, and I did just that in part through candid and frequent conversation with those under my supervision. We met weekly as a team to discuss touchpoints with our clients. I also initiated monthly learning sessions so that we could discuss our highlights and low points of the month.

The following is a summation of my duties while working as an HR Director:

- Responsible for organizational effectiveness and human resources generalist support of broadcast engineers, enterprise applications developers, digital media enterprise engineers and developers, strategic audience strategist and technology operations

- Responsible for a staff of eight human resource professionals supporting 2,800 employees reporting to the Senior Vice President of Human Resources, International and Technology Operations

- Create change management training and develop comprehensive change management tools; research and recommend organizational development strategies to be adopted for software engineers, developers, and broadcast engineers to develop members of client groups from functional leaders to leaders of people in the organization; recommendations were implemented

- In conjunction with the recruiting team, create strategies for hiring, placement, and retention for talent across the technology organization

- Partner with internal and external resources on the design, development, and delivery of functional/technical leadership training

But remember that weeds grow in the fertile soil along with the seeds, a truth I was reminded of when I became entangled in controversy despite celebrating significant success at this corporation. The turmoil was once again tied to the actions of a specific individual who in this instance sent an anonymous letter internally to the Chief Human Resources Officer, who was the supervisor to my boss. Her purpose was to lambast my abilities and question why I was given such a significant role in the organization. I learned years later that a Black female who happened to be one of my direct reports sent the scathing epistle in which she specifically stated that my character flaws made me an unbecoming leader. Among the sins cited was the claim that I cursed at my staff members, frequently smoked cigars, and openly discussed my romantic rendezvous in such detail that my conversation became inappropriately and uncomfortably sexually explicit.

I was blindsided and mortified. While it is true that I have been known to add expletives to my sentences, I use such language to express that I have reached a boiling point over a situation versus a person. I do not swear at individuals, which I consider a very improper and unproductive way to engage in conversation with another person. Walls go up and solutions disappear when leadership takes that approach as a management strategy.

I could not deny the fact that I will on occasion smoke a cigar, which I realize is surprising to those who know me as the woman influenced by a grandmother who preached to present in a proper fashion. I have been described as the consummate professional who is always impeccably dressed and in fact, I work to consistently present myself as ready for the next level up in position and title. It is for that reason that I am very cautious as to when I indulge in a cigar and carefully choose the company I am with when I light a stogie. The final accusation that I improperly boasted about exploits with men would have been laughable in any other context. I was in the early stages of rebuilding after a failed marriage and was void of any interest in a relationship. To put it bluntly, I had no sex life to discuss!

Feeling certain that my future in this organization was doomed, I went to the CHRO and offered my resignation. I did so not because I was feeling any guilt about wrongdoings or had regret for the way in which I had managed my team. I was in defense mode, determined to take whatever action was needed to protect my image and reputation. There was a sense of relief when I was told to stay in my position and instead of quitting, write a rebuttal. And so I did, which had a catharsis effect but was not enough for me to completely overcome a lack of trust

The following is a summation of my duties while working as a Vice President of HR:

- This role had wide-ranging human resources strategy for the company's Global Technology Operations division, which included Audience Multi-platform Technologies, Global Network Operations, Technology Development and Services, Systems Technology and Engineering.

- In this capacity, I was responsible for partnering with the key executives in technology to create and implement key business initiatives as well as planning and recommending human resources strategies to build individual and organizational capability.

- This role managed a team of HR professionals and together, we supported several hundred employees.

I developed in some of my employees and coworkers. I also became increasingly cynical about the organization as a whole, isolating myself as much as possible as I intensified my efforts to do my best work.

I saw renewing my commitment to excellence as a way to shut out the draining noise that was once again blasting all around me. A benefit to the approach was that soon after the letter episode, I was chosen for a promotion. What made this raise especially joyous was that I finally reached the point in my career where I was a vice president. The opportunity came after four years in the media conglomerate and as I was contemplating how long I could tolerate staying given the anonymous attack on my character and credentials. I count this opportunity to move up one more rung on the corporate ladder while in the middle of turmoil as another example of the rewards that come through perseverance. My goal at that point was frankly to get out of the company but instead, I was elevated into a higher leadership rank.

The focus of the vice president position was to bring together a team to provide first-class service to the client we supported.

During the two years that I served in this role, I was blessed to complete a lengthy international assignment, which is discussed in Chapter 9. While working in the U.S., I found the responsibilities to be demanding but exhilarating. There was a sense of fulfillment as I had reached a significant milestone in my career. Because I had decided to stay, I became the heir apparent for the Senior Vice President position. This was the natural progression in the company that I had served for six years. I anticipated the transition would come through a promotion without a cumbersome and unnecessary search process.

Instead of celebrating the expected promotion, I resigned. I realized I could no longer stay with the company when I was told that I would need to submit an application for the position as if I were an unknown, external candidate. The fact that my counterparts in the firm did not have to post for the positions they were promoted into was yet another example of inequitable treatment, a blatant slight that I could not ignore. Convinced it was time to exit, I handed my letter of resignation to the CHRO. She was shocked, noting that it was expected I would want the Senior Vice President job. My response was that had the value I added to the organization over the years been recognized and my accomplishments appreciated, there would be no need to go through the application process to acquire the position I had earned through past performance. My words were as clear as my message: I was not going to be disrespected or dismissed. I also was not going to stay put or stay quiet.

LESSONS LEARNED

Situated prominently in my office is a quote that reads, *They told me I couldn't. That's why I did.* I hope you noticed that it is included at the start of this book. These words have become my mantra and frankly, they succinctly reveal how I have stayed upright while moving upward in all I have endeavored—from marriage to graduate school and as I blaze my trail in Corporate America. In each of these separate worlds, I have encountered and endured negative behavior tied to the repeated efforts of someone trying to put me in my place. Whether it came from a disgruntled spouse, a punitive professor, or a colleague in a dysfunctional workplace, I have been told repeatedly and bluntly that I am not enough of whatever is required or desired. Not committed enough. Not emotional enough. Not enough positive traits or abilities to be a leader.

What I realized when I went through the season where it seemed persecution persisted on all sides was that I held the ultimate power because I was in complete control of how I responded. Embracing the negativity and believing my critics were right to doubt my abilities and aspirations was certainly one option. In one sense that is the easier choice, as the only requirement is to accept the idea that failure is inevitable. That leads to insurmountable self-doubt that results in giving up on yourself and your dreams.

I instead made the conscious choice to silence my doubters and critics by pushing forward until I found success, which has convinced me that the best revenge truly is doing well and looking good as you excel. Each prediction of defeat felt like I was being dared to go out and achieve what was presumably beyond my reach. Every toxic comment and negative experience made me more determined to break free and soar higher. For me, that resulted in leaving a miserable marriage, finishing my doctoral degree, and literally walking away from work environments where I was attacked or stifled or both.

I should explain that I worked to stay humble while enduring the setbacks in each situation, especially once I had overcome the obstacles. For example, I do not wear my Ph.D. credential as a badge, nor do I ask others to address me using the title of "Dr." I did the work so that when necessary, I can flex the fact I have added expertise gained through a rigorous education. There are situations where the clout tied to having a doctorate is essential in order for my voice to be heard, but it is not my nature to boast or behave in a way others may feel belittled.

I have found my inner strength by accepting the truth that there is a time to fight when forging your way forward in Corporate America. The key is to have a purpose to the fight, meaning you are putting your energy into clearing a path to enable progress versus becoming as abhorrent as the individuals who are your tormentors. To keep the right attitude and maintain positive energy when you are battling through those difficult days, you need to have a clear understanding of what defines, identifies, and motivates you. Keep that list cemented in your mind and use it to evaluate every decision, both personal and professional.

You will find it much easier to identify your niche and recognize your talents when you have a clear vision of who you are and where you are headed. Honestly evaluate if you are lacking a skill to reach your destination, then take steps to add it to your toolbox. Perhaps most importantly, use your list to assess if a criticism is valid and may be applied in some constructive way even if it was delivered poorly. If there is no merit, consider it noise. Stop listening and do whatever is necessary to move forward.

Your ultimate goal is to never let the words or actions of others push you off your path, not even a loved family member. If I had taken to heart what I was being told by my ex-spouse or unsupportive faculty, I would not have a Ph.D. I would still be sitting stymied in stifling personal and professional situations where I was unappreciated and underachieving. One of the best ways to stay on track is to find supportive mentors and friends who will be an encouragement when your energy runs low and confidence wanes.

Determine to create and maintain a strong professional network for as my experience has proven, there is no way to anticipate the opportunities that will come to you through those you have partnered with at some point in your career. They are the ones you must turn to in those moments when you need to share the pain, which is inevitable as you experience growth. They will help you realize that on the other side of the agony is the opportunity to continue reinventing yourself as the person and leader you are destined to become, but only when and if you find a way to silence your naysayers.

5

CLIMBING THE CORPORATE LADDER

THERE ARE TWO KEY ASPECTS TO EVERY ASCENT: REALIZING THE risks involved and developing a strategy to minimize them. Both are perhaps best on display when observing a rock climber, especially those adventurists who are brave enough to tackle a cliff free solo. I find it absolutely terrifying to watch a person slowly creep up what appears to be a nearly vertical rock face without a team and using no protective equipment. No ropes and no option other than to reach the summit. They rely solely on their hands and feet to mount the peak, pushing themselves to exhaustion while on the brink of disaster and potentially death.

While rising to a higher position in Corporate America is thankfully not life-threatening, there is a similarity to the daring rock climber in that an element of risk exists and must be balanced against potential personal and professional gain. Even the best made plan cannot eliminate the angst that comes in trying to decide if and when to take the next step forward and up. Leaving a position too soon can be a blow that may be hard to recover from, just as transitioning to a different job without the assurance that the desired rewards will be reaped is a constant and inherent risk experienced on every rung of the proverbial ladder.

Just as often happens for the literal rock climber, the professional may need to move back down or shift laterally to find another way to reach new heights. That is exactly what I decided to do when leaving the media conglomerate for a position as an HR Vice President in a financial services organization. The move was undoubtedly questioned and deemed a mistake by the team members and management group I left behind, as I passed on the opportunity to become a Senior Vice President, opting instead to remain at the VP level but in a much smaller private equity company. This new position was, however, fascinating on many levels and provided the opportunity to support a leader who I consider a mentor to this day.

I began working for a person who viewed me as a true business partner and frequently made me feel as if I was his consiglieri. I became part of an executive cabinet he created that included only three others—his head of communications, head of finance, and chief of staff. He instilled in us the importance of partnership and how when one succeeds, all succeed. This thinking matched my belief that iron sharpens iron. In addition to gaining significant professional growth, while in this role I met the man who later became my husband. Any doubt I made the right decision to take a stand and walk away from the Senior Vice President position was erased as I gained amazing work experience and a new lease on my personal life.

Despite the assumption I am sure some made that I had reached a point of stagnation in my career, I entered another season of growth by joining the private company as it was attempting to go public. Having never been involved in such a significant corporate paradigm shift, I gained knowledge in a completely different realm of HR. Suddenly I was part of a management team deciphering and predicting how becoming a public entity would impact the company's culture. There was ongoing discussion about a breadth of topics ranging from the influence external shareholders would have on the firm's overall vision to potential changes needed in daily operations.

Just as the climber who makes a move parallel across the rock soon begins the ascent once again, I limited the time spent in the lateral position. After just 11 months, I received a call from a nonprofit agency in need of an HR executive. Beyond the thrill of once again being sought out for a position when I was not looking to change my employment, I was additionally flattered to realize that I was being brought in for consideration

---

The following is a summation of my duties while working as an HR Vice President:

- Accountable for providing consultation on human capital and organizational development strategies for colleagues within the financial services organization.

- Lead HR strategy by directing cross functional HR initiatives to support and influence functional, financial, and operational objectives.

- Leverage the support of the Global HR Teams across the company to include compensation, talent acquisition, talent management, employee relations, regional and service delivery to help lead change and drive organizational effectiveness and engagement.

The following is a summation of my duties while working as a Chief Human Resources Officer:

- Responsible for the leadership of the team managing the functions of human resources, including systems, compensation and benefits, compliance, training, employment policies and procedures

- Responsible in leading and implementation of talent selection and development, succession planning, risk management regarding employees and volunteers, and career path initiatives throughout the organization

- Serve as one of the primary staff roles in support of strategic board-level initiatives where talent and leadership are key drivers to success

after the search team was to the point of completing final interviews with the initial slate of candidates. Such moments of recognition are remarkable because they rebuild and replenish self-esteem and confidence levels, healing the bruises acquired while being battered and beaten down in previous hostile situations.

I felt grateful and energized when I decided to make the career move and was hired as the Chief Human Resources Office for the nonprofit organization in 2015. My sidestep proved to be a sound decision because I reached a new level of leadership with the CHRO title. I soon became immersed in the hardest job I had yet to tackle in my career, gaining enormous experience and satisfaction as a reward for managing difficult issues. The challenges were unique in that I had joined an organization that was focused on fulfilling a mission versus making money. What a radical shift from the days of implementing strategies with a corporate team driven by the imperative that the business earn a profit to reward investors. While all of the previous experiences prepared me for what I would learn in this position, I found that my girth and perseverance were tested as never before as

I learned more about myself as a leader and an HR professional than I ever could have imagined.

There were numerous new opportunities in my CHRO role, including partnering with an oversight board that consisted of corporate or civic leaders in significant leadership roles. I would never have had the experience of collaborating with such a team of accomplished professionals if I had not deviated to accept the nonprofit position. Board members were very supportive of my joining the agency, and I once again entered a stage of my professional life where I was sharpened by those surrounding me. The insights gained and friendships added were invaluable, including the opportunity to work with Richard Gerakitis. At that time, he was a managing partner for a law firm in Atlanta and chaired the board's HR committee. We consequently worked together frequently and developed a strong professional relationship that I continue to value today as he remains a close friend and confidante.

Board support proved to be vital as I faced significant and ongoing obstacles when attempting to make major changes to the agency's HR policies and procedures which, if they even existed, were archaic. For example, it was a surprise to realize that the organization was still using paper applications when recruiting. I consequently decided that one of my first efforts would be to update and improve the way the agency's HR office functioned overall. I introduced a Human Capital Management System to transform all of the traditional HR functions ranging from payroll and training to recruitment, compensation, and performance management.

The transition was arduous because so many staff were against change. What could have been accomplished in half a year took 18 months of hard work to complete the implementation, in part because the payroll director and chief financial officer partnered to put up every roadblock conceivable. I had never experienced such purposeful efforts to sabotage an initiative. They made no attempt to hide their complete disregard for me. The extent of discontent became even more apparent after I left the agency. It was then I learned from a colleague that the payroll director–a white female without a degree–brought a discrimination lawsuit against the agency after my hire in part because she did not appreciate reporting to me as Black female.

She was not the only individual within the organization who struggled with my presence. I soon realized the level of discontent and distrust centered around not only me but HR in general. Many questioned why a CHRO was needed and what good could be accomplished with the changes I was going to introduce. I felt a great need to prove myself and was somewhat confused by the reactions I encountered until the CEO provided the insight I was lacking. He made it clear that the agency did not fire employees. While the revelation was shocking, his words also brought a sense of relief. Suddenly it made sense as to why the changes I envisioned and championed sparked apprehension within the agency. I was going to put in place systems to evaluate a person's performance, create an improvement plan if needed, and issue a pink slip should the employee fall short of reaching the stated work goals.

I still marvel that the organization was functioning without setting expectations for the people in charge of fulfilling the mission and had no qualms about the fact there was no accountability for the quality of work being done or the level of productivity. Remember that I started my career with PepsiCo Inc. with managers who set a standard of excellence. I advanced to work at high-performing global organizations where each person's performance was key. The companies depended on dedicated and stellar employees who diligently supported the mission and wanted to contribute to the corporation's ongoing success. Given I had ingrained in me from my family and my earliest employers that the bar of excellence does not bend to mediocrity, the status quo at the nonprofit was not going to continue as long as I was the CHRO. I put into action my conviction that the agency had to set clear expectations for every person filling every position to reach and maintain a level of excellence that would permeate the agency's services and reputation.

I shared with Richard the fact that I was experiencing battle fatigue and gained career advice that I value yet today. He was always a great sounding board and consistently reminded me that I was picked for the role, I was more than capable, and I should be the one to hold the position. Whenever I had the privilege to spend time with him, his encouragement made me want to keep going. Having him as a confidante during the time I was growing in the CHRO position was a blessing, especially because he provided encouragement and assurances that the board was supportive of my work. While staff openly deemed my ideas radical and were never shy about expressing their disdain for the implemented improvements, the board was pleased and the CEO appreciated my work. He promoted me to the position of Executive Vice President/CHRO, increasing my responsibilities as I retained oversight of diversity and inclusion initiatives.

It had taken two decades but I reached the role of EVP, which had become one of my professional goals as I progressed in my career. I secured the position despite having to pass up the opportunity for the title in the previous company and taking a sidestep in a different organization to reach this next career pinnacle. I was invigorated and became even more committed to

The following is a summation of my duties while working as an EVP/CHRO:

- Responsible for leadership of the team, managing the functions of HR systems, compensation and benefits, compliance, training, employment policies and procedures
- Responsible for leading and implementing talent selection and development, succession planning, risk management regarding employees and volunteers, and career path initiatives throughout the organization
- Serves as one of the primary staff roles in support of strategic, board-level initiatives where talent and leadership are key drivers to success
- Provides strategic leadership to all DEI efforts within the organization

focusing on strategic personnel development, addressing how the changing workforce would impact the nonprofit, and building a team mindset across the organization that was still lacking in a basic understanding of the scope and significance of work done through Human Resources.

I had been in the field enough years to take for granted that the role of an HR professional was understood as foundational and appreciated as an essential aspect to any corporation as it achieved and maintained success. In the simplest of terms, I explain that HR is a strategic approach to "people capital." This means that the work of a professional in the field is far more involved than recruiting a strong and skilled workforce. The goal is to develop and manage the talent of all individuals so that they reach maximum job satisfaction, which in turn results in stellar performance that elevates the corporation or agency.

This nonprofit did not value HR in part because they saw the unit's work as merely a transactional function of bringing people into the agency. Given the leadership team and employees in general did not grasp the merit or purpose of my role, I set aside time to purposefully educate and explain what HR could accomplish as a division and what members of the HR team should be doing within that agency to support and advance the mission. One goal as EVP was to demonstrate the value of HR when the unit functions as it should in a broad sense—meaning tackling big-picture issues such as adding a focus on personal growth, addressing succession to guarantee stability, and introducing the value of DEI initiatives.

Beyond a lack of understanding and appreciation for HR as a unit within the agency, I also became painfully aware that many long-term employees did not trust me in the leadership position because I was a Black female. I consequently faced ongoing resistance regardless of the specific initiative. For example, another goal I established while serving as EVP was to strengthen the bond between coworkers. This became particularly difficult to achieve because of one vice president's conniving behavior that reinforced my growing concern about the behavior of women toward each other in the workplace.

Unlike other employment situations where I had encount— ered microaggressions or strategic, passive-aggressive actions meant to deflate me or derail implementation of a plan I was spearheading, this female colleague who was a direct report took the unique approach of working hard to befriend me. My initial response was a sense of gratitude, as I appreciated the fact that I was able to quickly connect with a leader on my team while settling into the elevated EVP role. Having another individual make the effort to build a strong relationship was encouraging and a boost of confidence. My appreciation for her frequent gifts and kind gestures soon turned to disgust, however, as I realized that she was attempting to create a bond with me to discourage her direct reports from making me aware of her behavior on the job. By appearing to be my close friend and trusted colleague, her staff quickly believed they could not approach me with their concerns about what was happening under her leadership.

This was a radically different experience from the attacks I had endured as I earned my doctorate or all the setbacks during my years of climbing the ladder in Corporate America. This situation felt even more egregious than the myriad painful words thrown at me and the appalling behavior of individuals in past positions who tried to persuade me into believing I was less than capable. I consequently paused for a period of reflection that involved introspection about what had transpired throughout my career.

I recounted the ways I had been denied equitable pay, be it with a lower salary than my peers or coworkers in lesser positions, or in terms of benefits provided to those with the same rank but that I did not receive. I remembered innumerable microaggressions that eroded my trust in leadership, including instances where colleagues intentionally downplayed my accomplishments and insulted me by using a lesser title to introduce or address me when my rank within the company was established and known.

I contemplated the endless hours put into achieving more than expected just to convince others in the corporation that I was worthy of a leadership role and had the skills required to complete the responsibilities that came with the position of power. I thought back to the toxic behaviors of so many individuals who made it clear their goal was to put me in my place, which they bluntly stated was anywhere but in a leadership role. I wrestled with the reality that even when I had been named to a position that was a part of the leadership team, I was often made to feel like the outsider whose opinion was not sought or appreciated.

I grimaced while remembering the conversation with a headhunter who was seeking a Black female to hold an executive position but was not convinced I was a big enough name for the role, only for me to eventually be hired in a comparable job. I cringed while recalling how I repeatedly had been put in a position of a forced apology upon the orders of a superior when I was the one with the grievance, or the times I was told to make a situation work with a colleague who purposefully prevented any level of a professional partnership.

Each memory reaffirmed that I was always in a fight. I understood anew why I consistently felt battle fatigue. But I also knew that exhaustion was not the reason I was unsettled by the female direct report attempting to quiet her team by creating the façade of a close friendship between us. The difference from this struggle and all the others was that I had been led to believe a relationship had been established. The fact that I felt duped on a personal level by another person attempting to gain a professional advantage was unnerving. Beyond renewing my need to remain vigilant when placing my trust in others, I came to the conclusion that it was once again time for me to take my talents elsewhere.

Leaving the EVP position was made easier by the fact that I joined the nonprofit knowing that it was never my intention to stay for an extended time. I maximized the opportunities to gain additional skills in a different realm during my four years with the organization and built my resume with duties completed in elevated roles from the titles I held at my previous places of employment. There was the added blessing of expanding my professional network with colleagues who remain important mentors and peers in my life today.

Uncertainty about where I would continue my career dissipated when I received a call from a woman who had been my superior while I worked at the media conglomerate. She was aware of a position with the Atlanta Braves and inquired as to my level of interest. My enthusiasm resulted in an interview within one week of the unexpected phone conversation. I met with members of the search committee filling the position of Senior Vice President/Head of Human Resources. They invited me in for consideration despite the fact the search had progressed to the point that finalists were being interviewed. The confidence I had gained from my years working as a Manager, Director, Vice President, Chief Human Resources Officer, and Executive Vice President prepared me for the position that I thankfully was offered. I was thrilled to join the Major League Baseball franchise in 2019.

I would not be truthful if I failed to confess that I initially dealt with some frustration in dropping from the EVP title back to the Senior Vice President level. It was a struggle to fight the feeling I had taken a professional step backward, a negative thought I overcame by reminding myself that I was transitioning into a corporate environment once again after serving in a nonprofit organization. Any qualms about my decision to drop down a step in my career climb quickly dissipated as I formed a strong working relationship with the President and CEO for the Braves. I had his full support and was welcomed as a strategic partner as I worked to implement strategies that would strengthen the HR functions for the organization that includes players, coaches, approximately 450 full-time employees and nearly 2,000 part-time, game-day staff.

In addition to hiring, training, and working to improve the experience for all employees, my duties involved managing the Braves Development Company, which is a real estate development project that owns and operates The Battery Atlanta. A sports and entertainment destination, The Battery Atlanta is a two-million-square-foot venue situated adjacent to Truist Park, which is home to the Braves. I also had the personal task of adapting the skills I had acquired to fit within the new work environment of a sports entertainment business.

The challenge to acclimate was one I welcomed, as I had never worked in an organization with such a unique mission of delivering joy, camaraderie, and fun to a stadium and community filled with fans. There is an inherent energy that accompanies these goals, and I soon realized that working to provide such intangibles made every initiative feel a bit magical. There were many days when I looked out over the ballpark and remembered the excitement I felt as a little girl watching a baseball game with my grandparents. I still cherish that time from years ago. Having the opportunity to help create such moments that will become indelible memories for others is a privilege and added to my enthusiasm as I began working for the Braves.

I soon realized there is also plenty of stress that accompanies the job, as COVID-19 hit within months of my taking the position. Like the majority of individuals in leadership roles, I found myself navigating uncharted territory while dealing with a reduction in workforce and other significant organizational changes necessary as a result of the pandemic. Those of us working in the professional leagues had some unique challenges, as games were initially postponed or canceled and then scheduled but played without anyone in attendance. It was not until 2021 that fans were welcomed back to stadiums. The disruption sent shockwaves through the organization and was the first of many times my talents were tested while working for the Braves.

Despite the unexpected upheaval that resulted from COVID, I was able to bring some significant change as I began transforming the HR unit, now preferably referred to as the People Capital Department. Training programs and employee resource groups expanded the organization's culture and, through collaboration with my peers, an internal DEI Council was established with the goal of exploring social justice issues from the perspective of professional sports. The council gives employees a voice and initiates dialogue within the organization about important and often misunderstood aspects of diversity, equity, and inclusion. One example is the distinction between diversity and inclusion, which is how people see you versus having people make you feel welcome.

Much to my delight and surprise, I was promoted to serve as Executive Vice President/Chief People Capital Officer just 18 months after accepting the SVP position. Beyond the inspiring vote of confidence, the advancement elevated me to the title I had previously held. I was relieved to have affirmation that I had made the right career move, and I was excited to have the opportunity to continue the professional growth I was experiencing by taking on an expanded leadership role. My priorities included focusing on the company's people initiatives that involved employee engagement, leadership development, and performance management.

Working for the Atlanta Braves has provided the opportunity for me to experience many new firsts as I tackle challenges unique to the industry of professional sports. What I appreciate the most about the responsibilities is that there is a level of respect for the HR function and the strategic efforts undertaken by my team. I am at the point in my career where I am a leader whose voice is heard in the boardroom and whose opinion is valued as decisions are made. The extent to which my contributions are appreciated was cemented when one year after my promotion to EVP, my role was expanded exponentially yet again in 2022. Today I am the Executive Vice President/Chief Culture Officer for the Braves, which adds to my duties the handling of communications and community affairs in addition to the ongoing responsibilities already under my supervision. I lead the business/people strategy by delivering excellent HR services resulting in increased capability, as well as building high-performing, engaged teams and providing support to my leaders who are responsible for communications/public relations and community affairs.

The opportunity to become involved in the Atlanta Braves Foundation is one of the most rewarding aspects of my current position, as its purpose is to build community through baseball by activating the team's fan base to reach vulnerable populations. The goal is to improve equity and access in sport, health, education, and well-being outcomes for children, families, and communities. Specific objectives include establishing wellness programs that will include providing support for those battling cancer and life-altering illnesses, investing in teachers and students, addressing equity and access in baseball and softball, honoring those who serve in the community and creating more opportunities to volunteer, and caring for the environment while working to build a sustainable environment.

It is beyond invigorating and rewarding to be involved in such an outreach that is designed to empower and elevate individuals. The efforts align beautifully with the work I began decades ago in the field of Human Resources, which I entered with the goal of serving others as they strive to improve themselves personally and professionally. I was equally committed to continuing to grow myself and through the years, became increasingly determined to prove my abilities.

Today I am thriving at a leadership level that I did not initially envision as part of my life plan and later often doubted was feasible given the brutally negative feedback I consistently

The following is a summation of my duties while working as EVP/Chief Culture Officer for the Braves:

- Manage all communications for the Braves
- Oversight of all community affairs for the Braves
- Manage The Battery Atlanta
- Manage the team's spring training facility operations
- Continue to expand the organization's culture
- Continue to advance DEI initiatives
- Serve on the Atlanta Braves Foundation Inc. Board of Directors

received from naysayers. The persistent attacks that existed in every workplace became such substantial obstacles that I had reason to doubt I could take up one more step on the professional ladder. I relied on my cumulative educational and professional experiences to give me the confidence to keep climbing. What a joy to have reached the point in my career where I am reaping the benefits of my resilience and perseverance. I defied the odds. I unlocked the door to the C-Suite in Corporate America.

LESSONS LEARNED

There is a fine line between being a strong and independent person forging your path forward and becoming that foolish individual who believes there is no need for assistance on the climb up the corporate ladder. Straying too far in either direction is detrimental, as you do not want to be reliant on others to reach your goals, but you also cannot risk the inevitable failure that will come if you ignore the need for a team. Do not take the approach of the free solo climber but rather, continue to expand your network of mentors and peers who will advise, critique, encourage, create a refuge for safe conversation and emotional release, and unexpectedly unlock doors to opportunities you never envisioned. Equally important, become that reliable person to others who need you as part of their tribe. They too are seeking a safe haven with someone who will be there to provide words of wisdom when they feel frail from battle fatigue.

Give yourself permission to pause during the ascent. Exhaustion is unavoidable as you do the work to excel in Corporate America. There is no reason for worry or regret if you take a temporary retreat to recharge before surging upward. It is equally important to realize that strategy is essential to succeed in reaching your goals for without it, what was intended to be a brief rest can become a complete stop. Be pragmatic and keep an objective view of both your destination and plan to reach it. This empowers you to remain eager without becoming overwhelmed, equipped versus naïve about potential challenges and obstacles, and focused on the work at hand without feeling a sense of stagnation. Remember that the climber does not move until he can see a secure place to grab hold and pull up.

Be sure and include in your plan the possibility of taking a step back or down in order to continue your climb. As evidenced by my experiences, there are times when it is wise if not imperative to move laterally or lower before reaching a new professional height. There may be myriad reasons why such a shift is beneficial, from gaining experience in a different realm of work to taking a stand against an injustice occurring in your current place of employment. Tune out the noise from individuals who may assert you are making a mistake if you take a position with a lesser title or join a smaller organization. They do not understand that you are merely gaining a more solid footing before going higher.

Realize that reaching the pinnacle is not the end of your journey. While there is reason to feel a sense of pride and accomplishment, do not lose your humility because of what you have achieved or let your hunger to do more diminish. Use your position to empower individuals within your corporation and across your community. There are others still on the climb who need you to help lift them up. Continue to assess what remains on the horizon for yourself as well. There are always other mountains yet to be conquered. There are always more opportunities waiting behind doors that are not yet unlocked.

Me and Daddy (DeRay Cole) with me as a baby

Graduation from Douglasville Comprehensive High School,
Douglasville, GA, 1988

Me, Cole Paschall (Son) & Austin Paschall (Son)

Me and Daddy (DeRay Cole) at his book signing in Mooresville, SC

Me and Daddy (DeRay Cole) at my Ph.D.
commencement ceremony, 2010

Me, Mother (Fay Cole) and Papa (Cornelious Kelly)
at my Ph.D. commencement ceremony, 2010

Me and my Brother (Andre' Cole)

Me and former Ambassador to the United Nations Andrew Young at the National Center for Civil and Human Rights, Atlanta, GA, 2021

Me and former Secretary of State Condoleezza Rice at
The Masters at Augusta National, Augusta, GA, 2016

Speaking my TedTalk at TedX UGA, 2018

Me and Leon at our wedding at the
Ravenel Bridge in Charleston, SC, 2017

Me and Mother, 2019

Me in my regalia with Leon when I spoke to the Family and
Consumer Sciences graduates at University of Georgia-Athens

Me while on assignment in Hong Kong

Jordan Rhodes (Bonus Son), Leon Rhodes, Me, Austin Paschall & Cole Paschall in front of the Christmas tree at Rockefeller Center, NY, 2017

Cole Paschall, Jordan Rhodes & Austin Paschall in New York, 2017

Family picture 2019,
Seated: Austin Paschall & DeRay Cole
Standing: Cole Paschall, Me, Leon Rhodes, & Fay Cole

Family Holiday, 2021
Leon Rhodes & Jordan Rhodes

Family Holiday, 2021
Austin Paschall, Jordan Rhodes & Cole Paschall

Alpha Kappa Alpha, Inc. Sorority Luncheon, 2017
From left: Delisa Rodney, Fay Cole (Mother), Stacy Franklin,
Ladella Holmes, Kimberly Howard (Cousin), Me, Josyln
McGaughy (Cousin), and Yvonne Croswer Yancy

Me, 2024

6

TAKING THE HELM AS A
SERVANT LEADER

ANOTHER PARABLE I RECALL OFTEN, AND WHICH HAS BECOME MORE applicable in my life as I have advanced in my career, is that of a wealthy gentleman who was about to embark on a lengthy journey. Recorded in the New Testament book of Matthew, the story details how the man enlisted three of his servants to oversee his affairs while he was away, entrusting each with a sum of money in the form of a talent. Scholars believe a talent equated to 20 years of labor in biblical days. One of the men was given five talents, another two talents, and the third received one. The first two servants worked diligently and doubled the value of what they had been given, earning the praise of their master and gaining more responsibility. The third did nothing but protect his single talent so he could safely return it to his master, who was enraged and ordered a punishment because the servant made no attempt to be a good steward.

The message of this simple story reinforces the fact that each of us have unique skills and are blessed with opportunities to use our gifts in ways that are beneficial to others. There is the expectation that we will work with what we have been given and will reap rewards for the results of our diligent labor. I frequently reflect on the passage as a personal reminder that to whom much is given, much is expected. I have been the recipient of myriad opportunities and experiences to grow and advance. I consequently firmly believe that I am called to diligently produce and deliver what others need to succeed, especially my employer. The parable also serves as a vivid illustration that some workers are incapable of delivering results without explicit direction and careful supervision, which is a truth I also embrace as a leader.

Both themes conveyed in the biblical lesson are significant to me as someone who is now managing from the C-Suite. There are moments in each day that I contemplate some aspect of my professional journey and recognize anew the responsibility I have to use my talents in ways that will empower others while elevating the organization. I also realize that I need to be aware as I manage those under my supervision that each person has unique gifts and challenges, meaning the level of direction and oversight needed will vary based on the person and circumstance.

Given this is my perspective, it should not be surprising that I position myself to be a servant leader. I do not waiver from this philosophical approach as I handle my responsibilities in my current EVP/Chief People Capital Officer role, which is far more encompassing than the traditional CHRO duties. With each promotion my workload has expanded exponentially, as has the need for me to stay grounded in what I know to be best leadership practices. Today I have a team of 24 direct reports and supervise three departments that include communications, community affairs, and people capital, which incorporates all functions of a Human Resources unit.

My knowledge of how to lead has certainly been influenced by my studies, reinforced by my ongoing involvement and growth in professional organizations, enriched by my mentors, and sharpened by each new initiative undertaken. There is no doubt in my mind, however, that my style and priorities as a manager and decision-maker have evolved because of the lessons I learned while climbing the ladder in Corporate America. I trained under and partnered with individuals who have brilliant minds and an equally bright spirit. They taught me through word and deed what it takes to be a respected and effective leader in a business environment. They challenged my thinking, facilitated my growth, put my setbacks in perspective, and ultimately positioned me to be the leader that I am today. Beyond my commitment to doing my best in every job regardless of the time and energy required, I have risen to my current role because I have been supported, mentored, and prepared for success by amazing people and as a result of extraordinary experiences.

As noted in the previous chapters, I have also encountered hurdles, headaches, and haters along my academic and professional path. The knowledge gained from the recurring deflating situations I survived has been just as valuable if not more so in shaping how I approach every leadership opportunity that comes my way. I mention the struggles yet again because all too often as I partner with new colleagues, engage in community activities, serve on boards, and speak before audiences, I meet individuals who mistakenly insinuate that I have had an easy rise to the C-Suite. Hell no! I am quick to correct their thinking and politely dispel that notion as being far from the truth.

Others will offer sincere praise as they comment on my accomplishments and how I have become so successful. While grateful for the compliments, I again respond by sharing a reality about how I perceive myself. Rather than boast about how high I have climbed in Corporate America, I comment on the fact that I have worked diligently my entire life to maximize every opportunity and am blessed to reap the rewards for my exhausting labor. For while they may see me as the upper-echelon executive who is part of a powerful corporate team, I honestly still often envision myself as the child wearing pigtails while visiting with her grandparents in Arkansas. I am the teenage girl anchored by the family foundation that I built my future upon, and I am still that young adult determined not to fail.

What I am not is my job or my professional title. Such a statement may startle some, but I am determined to always present as a complete person versus merely the position that is printed on my business card. I firmly believe that choosing to identify by your work or title diminishes who you are as an individual and can be so limiting as to become crippling. I am constantly cognizant of the fact that I could lose my job and the accompanying title tomorrow. I am merely leasing whatever position I hold at any given time, as the office and the duties will exist long after I depart. Embracing this truth keeps me attentive to all aspects of my life, not just the professional roles I fill, and motivates me to maintain a healthy work-life balance.

When on the job, however, I am completely focused on the task at hand. Those who know me best in my professional role will describe me as a leader who is skilled, decisive, consistent, and truthful. Others have stated that I am transparent, determined, tireless, driven, and compassionate. My personal goal is to always include humility in that list of desirable traits, as I never want to reach a point in my career or personal life where I deem myself greater than the person standing nearby. I know from my own experiences that arrogant leaders never succeed in building a cohesive team eager to support initiatives, nor are they capable of creating a healthy work environment.

While I have more responsibility than the team I lead, I want each member of my staff to know that their skills and contributions are as critical to the organization's success as the work I complete. This requires that every individual be centered in the knowledge of who they are and know with certainty the attributes they bring to the team. With that as a foundation, my goal becomes to create an office culture where every staff member knows I will never ask more of them than I expect from myself, and I will not leave them to stand alone in the middle of a mess.

They have this assurance because I consistently preach specifically how we as a team will function together within the corporation. I expect each of my employees to embrace the concept that as a team, we have a brand that we must project and protect. Our specific unit's brand, which impacts all that we attempt and accomplish as a team, has eight elements that I emphasize are mandatory for each member to embrace and personify. They succinctly describe what is expected of each employee in terms of skill level, attitude, and approach to the work assigned.

To demonstrate the importance of working as a team united through a mutual commitment to the same standard of excellence, I share with my employees the idea of us all working in a foxhole. This is not to imply that we have a common enemy, but rather whatever challenge comes at us will be conquered because we

---

The following is the list of eight traits that are expected of all my employees.

- Be a consultant and business partner
- Be a service provider
- Become a subject matter expert
- Realize you are part of the organization's nucleus or conscience
- Be a people champion
- Serve as an influencer of the corporate culture
- Be a provider of guidance
- Be a trusted adviser

---

will be united and push through to a successful outcome. I preach collaboration and the truth that none of us stand alone, nor should we. The initiatives and issues we address are complex and fluid. It takes input from everyone to decipher a situation, decide on a course of action, and implement a plan to completion. I want to brainstorm with individuals who have varied backgrounds and perspectives because that is the best scenario for creative thinking and problem-solving. With this approach as common practice, my team knows they can call on the person to their right or their left and find a professional partner ready to engage and deliver.

Working for one another as opposed to just with each other also guarantees that there is no friendly fire in the proverbial foxhole. I have been in workplaces where I have been attacked by the person who was supposed to be my professional partner. The experience went beyond a counterproductive act that slowed progress on a company initiative to becoming a personal blow that left me feeling battered, bruised, and battle fatigued. I consequently enforce Standards of Operational Excellence that emphasize the need for cohesiveness within the team despite differences of opinion.

The following is a summation of the Standards of Operational Excellence model that I use as one of my leadership tools.

Operational Excellence is our commitment to doing the best job possible, always trying to improve to get to the next level, and taking the time to do things right no matter how big or small the task. Seamless execution is the goal.

Client Engagement

- Respond to emails/voicemails within 24 hours
- Own your role and responsibilities
- Become a subject matter expert in your role
- Be courteous and professional to team members and clients, always working collaboratively
- Provide full disclosure in all matters
- Meet expectations consistently and in a timely manner

Team Collaboration

- Be where you say you are going to be
- Seek to understand before being understood
- Address any issues as they occur between you and your team members or clients
- Always lead with positive intent
- Be transparent with openness, communication, and accountability, operating in such a way that it is easy for others to see what actions are performed
- Formally acknowledge and appreciate an achievement, service, or ability
- Operate as one team
- Have each other's back

Execution

- Ensure data is accurate, reliable, consistent
- Improve and increase capabilities through education and training opportunities in the workplace, through outside organizations, attending
- conferences and informal learning opportunities situated in practice
- Continually look for ways to become more efficient within your role and our HR processes and practices
- Be proactive

This is not to say conflict never arises. When it does, I encourage my employees to follow what I call the Pinch Theory. The idea is that there are two possible outcomes when a pinch occurs, meaning a problem exists between coworkers. How the situation is resolved depends on which path the individuals involved decide to pursue. One option is to avoid addressing the conflict, meaning the offense festers to the point hostility mounts and there is ultimately an inappropriate response. This mishandling typically results in corrective action that could potentially include termination. A better approach is to address the grievance directly with a personal conversation between the two employees who are at odds. Hopefully that action will result in reconciliation and restore a sense of camaraderie. If not, mediation begins with the goal of a plan being created so that both employees can find a way to productively coexist in the workplace.

Having been left to fend for myself too often in the past when I faced a hostile work situation, I gladly engage with employees who are struggling to overcome an issue. I speak with them individually and ask questions about the situation. Gathering information is important because assumptions are always detrimental. If the two cannot come together on their own, I will mediate and I will find a way for them to continue working as productive team members. They may never form a friendship, and that is not a problem because bonding at a personal level is not the goal. They just must find a way to work together productively and professionally. This is just one example of how I manage with a situational leadership style. By this I mean that I work to value the uniqueness of each individual. I also realize the correct response to a situation requires consideration of the personalities involved and details of the scenario, both of which are constantly changing variables.

I always want to understand each employee's specific circumstances, including personal situations if they wish to share. I will meet each person where they are and find a way to go forward, as I know from my own struggles while working through the drama I experienced during the divorce and graduate school that life events impact perspective and performance. I am convinced the best managers are capable of demonstrating empathy and understanding while still holding their employees accountable.

Combining compassion with directives is just one way I serve my employees, who I passionately protect. I argue that a leader should block and tackle within the organization so that the job is easier for the individuals they manage. I will be the fall person if one is needed, the sacrificial lamb so that my employees feel safe to take appropriate risks as they embrace new professional challenges. Another way I instill confidence in my team members is to offer sincere praise and recognition frequently and publicly. My mantra is to recognize openly and provide feedback privately. I do not take the credit for the exceptional work done by the team, and I do not fall apart when there is failure. I want the employees I lead to know I understand that on some occasions, we will miss the mark and fall short of our objective. The goal is always to fail in a small sense versus overall and fail fast, meaning we will not dwell on the negative but get back to work and right the wrong.

One of my most challenging and significant tasks as an EVP is to carefully select the right combination of talent so that failures are increasingly infrequent. When the need arises to add an employee to the team, I seek an individual who is skilled and committed to working collaboratively. The best candidate is a lifelong learner who is eager to develop further as a person and a professional. The ability to work in a fast-paced environment is critical, as is a high level of motivation. This is necessary because I am not a micro-manager. Having worked for supervisors who were, I know that style of leadership does not instill a sense of confidence or enthusiasm for the job.

I am equally diligent in a search when I am the one contemplating a new position, as I carefully assess if the organization and the CEO I will report to are a good fit for me as the employee. I have created a checklist for myself that details what I desire in my supervisor, with respect for what I bring to the table my top priority. I want to know that my experiences and talents will be valued. I also need to be in a professional partnership where there is an open dialogue built on mutual trust. Autonomy is equally essential, which I realize is contingent upon me building a reputation as the executive who delivers what is promised and consistently shows up with solutions followed by wins. I have established such a record throughout my career, in part because I spend significant time contemplating how I perform not only as the leader but as an employee.

My supervisors soon realize that I am a decisive person who is also pensive. They can know with certainty that the plans I pitch and solutions I suggest have been analyzed by me to evaluate potential blowback and pitfalls. I will have studied the scenario extensively and be able to present the pros and cons of every possible approach. I am also always proactively informing. My goal is to make certain that my CEO is never blindsided, which is one of many ways I build trust in my leadership skills. Being able to perform and deliver during those occasions when a firestorm does erupt is equally important. When those situations arise, I remain calm as I assess the situation to identify the problem and then develop a plan so the needed action can be taken immediately and the issue will be resolved quickly.

The fact that I function well when in crisis mode without high emotion is recognized and appreciated by my supervisors. They know that I will never show up as the Chicken Little character with my hair on fire and frantic because the sky is falling. My ability to remain calm and motivate the team to find solutions versus becoming so emotional that panic ensues is a skill I learned as a child. I credit my father for teaching me that tears are not a productive response when hard times hit. He would consistently ask why I was crying and remind me that I would never solve anything by sitting in a puddle of my tears. I learned the lesson so well that remember my ex-husband called me "Ice Princess." While deemed a negative in my first marriage, I have found the ability to control my emotions to be a highly beneficial and valued skill in Corporate America.

I believe it is imperative for me as a leader to not only have the ability to deal with the situation at hand in a controlled manner and be effective in the moment, but also always be thinking forward. This empowers me to pivot easily, as I am rarely caught off guard when a situation changes so that an initial solution is no longer valid or the best option. I am not flustered if Plan A or Plan B need to be scrapped because I come to the table with Plans A through J. My CEO also knows that I am capable of rallying my team to execute the directives attached to whatever decision is made, as I have proven my ability to motivate and guide employees so that their energy and stellar efforts guarantee the corporation's success.

One additional priority I have established for myself as both the employee and the leader is to strive for consistency. I want my bosses and team members to be so in tune with my thinking that they can predict what my answer will be before I join the conversation. It is also imperative that they realize I will speak truth regardless of how painful the words may be to hear. This once again ties to my message that courage of voice is essential to find success in Corporate America. I am passionate about the importance of finding your voice and have learned through my years in the field that an effective HR executive cannot succeed without having the courage to speak.

Because of my position, there are frequently occasions when I must provide a perspective that may not be favorable or liked. The end result is that I often find myself in fierce conversations, not in the sense that they are hostile but rather so painfully blunt or centered around such a difficult topic that they can become unpleasant. In all candor, I recall numerous occasions throughout my career when I was anxious if not close to fearful before engaging in conversations with my superiors who I knew would not be pleased by the message I was about to deliver. I also know that as the head of HR, it is my responsibility to be the watchdog over what is any corporation's most valuable and expensive asset, namely its employees. I now have the confidence in myself and my abilities to speak boldly, even if doing so means I temporarily find myself in the proverbial hot seat. I consider it just another essential part of my job as I fulfill my duties as a servant leader.

LESSONS LEARNED

Looking in at the life of a C-Suite executive, there is the impression that the job is filled with perks that make the work plush. There is some truth to that perception, as I will readily agree my office is oversized with a lovely view and flying on a corporate jet always beats the hassle of the commercial airline experience. What the outsider fails to consider, however, is that the responsibility that comes along with the EVP title and positions above are weighty and continuous. I am never afforded the luxury of turning off from work mode, which is without a doubt the most stressful aspect to serving at the top in Corporate America.

I have learned one way to manage the stress is to have outlets that introduce an element of relaxation. Increasingly, I actively nurture all aspects of my life. Exercise is important, which is why I make a commitment to attend Pilates classes as a way to strengthen my body and renew my mind. I also purposefully schedule personal time and social activities even when I am tempted to remain focused on a pressing work deadline. There is nothing more enjoyable or important than being with my husband Leon and our three sons. They are my top priority followed by reconnecting with others for anything but a work project. Whether attending an artistic performance, joining in a volunteer effort, or rekindling friendships with my sorority sisters, I find that managing stress is easier when I am intentional about balancing my work-life schedule.

I also buy shoes. When I am stressed, shoe shopping has an excellent cathartic effect. I do not mean dropping into a store for a few minutes on my way home after enduring a rough day that has left me feeling drained. I am talking a *Sex in the City* shoe shopping experience. Shoes are so important that when moving into my current Atlanta home, I had a California closet created to store and display them in an orderly fashion so the perfect pair for a specific outfit is easily within reach. I could argue that the goal of having an expansive shoe collection is to always present myself in the best possible light with a polished look, which is definitely a part of my plan to succeed as an executive. But the truth is that searching for shoes brings me momentary relief from the load I carry as a top corporate executive. Looking good is just an added benefit! I tell others who ask how they can handle the stress they experience on the job to find their equivalent to my buying shoes.

Another lesson I have learned as a leader is that managing my time is as crucial as managing my team. My schedule is frankly ridiculous, which is why it is imperative that I have a structure that I strictly enforce. For example, I start each workday meeting with my assistant. Twice a month I meet individually with each person who reports to me so that my finger is always on the pulse of all that is happening in each area I supervise. I also regularly meet with employees who report to my team leaders. Their voices also need to be heard. To avoid feeling overwhelmed by the multiple demands on my time each day, I use a color-coded calendar that helps me evaluate how well I am balancing all aspects of my life. Work commitments are in blue, board tasks are in yellow, speaking engagements are in orange, purple is for peer leadership meetings, and light green is a personal social activity. I encourage you to develop and rely on such a system to keep a grasp on your daily schedule.

Perhaps the most important requirement for a leader to remain successful in Corporate America is to develop and implement a personal management style that is positive so that employees are able to function productively in a healthy work environment. Doing so ensures you are a good steward who is maximizing your talents while drawing them out of others under your direction. For me, embracing the role of a servant leader has proven to be a successful way to enrich and empower those on my team so that they are capable of delivering their best effort. This perspective of my role makes me both an effective leader and valuable employee because I am able to consistently provide what my CEO needs in order for the organization to flourish.

Realize that regardless of how you choose to lead, speaking truth boldly is a key requirement to fulfill your responsibilities. While I have discussed in previous chapters the need for your voice to be heard in order to obtain what you personally need to advance in your profession, it is equally imperative that you become the leader in your corporation who speaks candidly when complicated issues and uncomfortable situations arise. It is an essential part of your job to be the courageous voice.

7

ADDRESSING CORPORATE
AMERICA'S CRIPPLING FLAW

T HERE NEEDS TO BE AN ADDENDUM TO THE ADAGE THAT A PICTURE is worth a thousand words, given numbers can also quickly and succinctly convey an enlightening story. Consider as an example the statistics tied to the presence of women in Corporate America and the amount of power they hold—or more importantly, the lack thereof—based on their position in the workplace. The numbers reveal a startling truth, and frankly an appalling trend, that has been sustained across generations.

A report released by the global nonprofit Catalyst in February 2023 documents that white women were 59.2 percent of the female population in the United States in 2021. Minority women that same year were 38.7 percent of the total. The minority cohort includes Hispanic/Latina, Black, and Asian representatives. The same report by the agency that states its mission is "to accelerate progress for women through workplace inclusion" predicts that by 2060, white women will represent 44.3 percent of the U.S. population and minority women's percentage will increase to 51.7.

Understand that this confirms a paradigm shift is occurring in this country, as women of color are projected to be the majority of all females in the United States within four decades. How women appear in the corporate workplace was also analyzed in the Catalyst document, which revealed that white women held 29 percent of entry-level positions in 2022, with 21 percent advancing to the C-Suite. Compare this to women in the minority cohort, who represented 19 percent of the low-level, entry jobs. Only 5 percent persevered to rise to a top executive position.

A report by *CNN Business* released in February 2021, two years earlier than the Catalyst study, affirmed that little progress has been made for women seeking a leadership role in Corporate America and that any improvement is achieved in minuscule increments. This truth is confirmed by the article that summarizes an investigation into Black women making history as top corporate leaders. *CNN Business* found that only 3.3 percent of all U.S. executive and senior leadership positions were filled by Black females in 2018. Equally alarming is the fact that since the names of Fortune 500 CEOs were first published by *Fortune* magazine in 1955, only 20 Black individuals have risen to be included in the list. There have been 17 men and three women, with Rosalind Brewer the most recent addition when she became Walgreens' CEO in March 2021. It should be noted that she left that position within three years.

Now consider that the first corporations to be established in the United States came into existence in the 1790s. The Boston

Catalyst provided a snapshot of how women are represented in Corporate America with the release of a research summation in February 2023. They reported that "from entry-level position to the C-Suite, the share of women of color in leadership remains small."

At the start of 2022, women of color held 19 percent of entry-level positions. Few advanced to leadership.

- Managers: 14%
- Directors/Senior Managers: 10%
- Vice Presidents: 8%
- Senior Vice Presidents: 6%
- C-Suite Positions: 5%

This compares to the following statistics that represent white women in the workplace as 2022 began. They held 29 percent of entry-level positions, with a higher percentage advancing to leadership roles.

- Managers: 27%
- Directors/Senior Managers: 26%
- Vice Presidents: 24%
- Senior Vice Presidents: 23%
- C-Suite Positions: 21%

Manufacturing Company, dating back to 1813, is documented to be one of the country's first industrial enterprises. At its peak, a workforce of approximately 300 employees relied on spinning and weaving equipment powered by water to create cotton textiles. Note again that date of 1813, which tells us Corporate America has been in existence for more than two centuries. During that time, the percentage of women in the nation has grown to more than half the population. And yet, women in general are rarely afforded the opportunity to serve in top leadership positions and Black women specifically are scarcely ever welcomed into the C-Suite.

I come to two conclusions when analyzing this disheartening data: Corporate America has a flaw that cripples itself and individuals, and I am part of a very small percentage of Black female executives. I am tied to a startling and infuriating statistic.

My lens is very clear as I look at Corporate America from the inside out. I see failure with regard to prioritizing the pursuit of women and capitalizing on the intelligence, perspective, and talent they bring to any organization. Realize that silencing women by the very fact they are not present in the boardroom, participating in strategic conversations, or given the opportunity to lead means that the perspective tied to half of the nation's population is not being heard. In addition, those who have persisted and taken their place in a company's upper echelon are not equitably compensated in comparison to their male peers.

There is also an internal angst women battle that can hinder their performance in the workplace, namely fear. Former chief operating officer for Meta Platforms and Facebook, Sheryl Sandberg, asserts that "fear is at the root of so many of the barriers that women face. Fear of not being liked. Fear of making the wrong choice. Fear of drawing negative attention. And the holy trinity of fear: The fear of being a bad mother/wife/daughter." Sandberg knows all too well the need to battle such emotion, as she also served as vice president of Global Online Sales and Operations at Google and has since founded LeanIn. Org to encourage and empower women.

My own professional journey has made me keenly aware that Black women carry an even more staggering burden than their white female peers while trying to break down locked doors that halt their professional progression. I obviously do not need to read investigative reports or scholarly assessments of the status of Black women in the workplace to realize I am part of a tiny cohort that has defied the odds to reach the C-Suite. I know this from observation and experience, as I have been battling at every stage of my career to achieve the next promotion. I have been very aware since completing my dissertation and taking my first HR job decades ago that the ceiling I would have to break through to secure an executive position in Corporate America was constructed of concrete versus glass.

Smashing it has been an exhausting process, requiring that I show up better prepared and more confident with more degrees than others in the candidate pool or those seated around the table. Even having completed the Ph.D. was not enough in my mind, which is why I pursued other leadership programs to further enhance my learnings, including Leadership Atlanta and the Women on Board cohort. I understand the need to provide substantial proof of being exceedingly capable. The reality regarding what would be demanded of me to excel was forewarned by my family, mentors, and coworkers. I quickly realized with disdain that the effort required of me to even be considered for any position would be more than what was expected from other employees. Why? Not just because I am a woman, but because I am a Black woman.

In order for there to be meaningful change and a positive shift in Corporate America for women, and especially minority females, it is imperative that there be a greater level of understanding about the struggles they fight to overcome. The obstacles, as detailed in the Black Woman Employee Lifecycle, are all too often universal. Knowledge is the first step toward action.

I know beyond any doubt that Black women encounter more than the typical stereotypes projected onto all women who are often perceived as being too emotional to lead, too burdened by family responsibilities that inherently fall to the female to be reliable and effective, or too lacking in experience or education to have the skills required for an executive role. Black women also frequently contend with another misperception that they are angry individuals who cannot be relied upon with certainty to be the cordial, productive team player. They are frequently

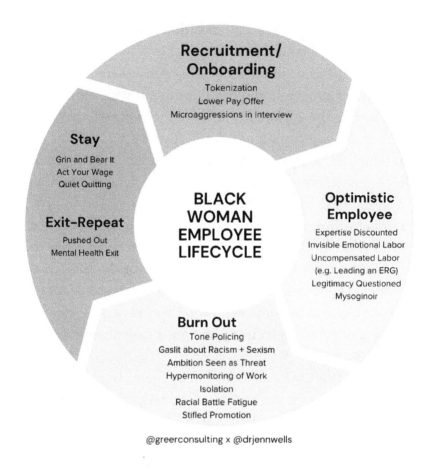

Recruitment/
Onboarding
Tokenization
Lower Pay Offer
Microaggressions in Interview

Stay
Grin and Bear It
Act Your Wage
Quiet Quitting

Exit–Repeat
Pushed Out
Mental Health Exit

BLACK
WOMAN
EMPLOYEE
LIFECYCLE

Optimistic
Employee
Expertise Discounted
Invisible Emotional Labor
Uncompensated Labor
(e.g. Leading an ERG)
Legitimacy Questioned
Mysoginoir

Burn Out
Tone Policing
Gaslit about Racism + Sexism
Ambition Seen as Threat
Hypermonitoring of Work
Isolation
Racial Battle Fatigue
Stifled Promotion

@greerconsulting x @drjennwells

and quickly labeled as a bitch when taking an appropriate stand in the workplace regardless of the situation.

Black women also have the heavier burden of adding the element of race to their gender as they walk the halls of Corporate America. They carry a constant awareness of both traits in the workplace and are challenged to maintain their identity while simultaneously finding a way to succeed in their career. The end result is dualism, which involves navigating different cultures and ultimately forces Black females to live different lives. For example, they work, live, and socialize in unique spaces that require them to engage in splicing as they show different parts of who they are based on the situation, circumstances, and those present.

For minority women such as myself who have had the perseverance, support, and opportunity to rise in Corporate America, there is the feeling of heavy responsibility to represent and elevate our gender and race. This is an inevitable burden because there are still so few others in our cohort who have found their place in the corporate world. One constant I have experienced throughout my career regardless of the position I held or organization where I worked is that it is a challenge to find Black women in positions of power. Trust me when I tell you the statistics are true! There is the perception that Black women cannot advance beyond a certain level. I have found that Black women, including myself, consequently feel that they are either isolated or diminished with no voice.

Why do I still battle such negative sentiments on occasion despite my proven record and current EVP position? Is it oftentimes because I'm the only female in the room, or is it because I'm typically only the Black female in the room? There are times I have had to look and say *Can you hear me? I matter!* I encounter constant reminders that there will always be some who question the necessity of my presence and demand that I prove my abilities yet again. This remains true even though I have reached a point in my career where I walk into the room knowing I have credibility and am certain beyond doubt that I am an expert in my field. And yet, I still encounter situations where others send the message by both word and deed that I am inadequate.

For example, I recall not that many years ago when I was in a meeting with two males from outside my organization. As we were talking, they asked who would be making the decision regarding the issue we were working to resolve. I stated that I held that authority and yet, they proceeded to explain that they would appreciate having my male peer become involved in the conversation. This initial insult was compounded when they asked for me to schedule a time they could meet with the preferred man. I know other women can relate as they have experienced equally belittling scenarios that at best only momentarily fuel self-doubt.

Consistently dealing with others who attempt to diminish me in some way, be it overtly or in a subtle manner, results in battle fatigue as I have discussed in earlier chapters. It also inevitably stirs the need to fight feeling like an imposter. Even today, with my record of successful and steady progression in different areas of Corporate America, I experience such powerful emotions on occasion. Despite the fact I am sitting in the C-Suite as an Executive Vice President who is respected and recognized as skilled based on the results of my work and numerous external accolades, I fight the monster that attacks every woman at some point in her career. I wonder if I belong.

Imposter syndrome is critically important to the conversation about the limited presence and role of women in Corporate America because while it may not impact the initial hiring of females, I am confident it is a factor in explaining why more do not persist and rise to prominence. Women battling imposter syndrome feel like a fraud or phony playing a role far beyond their abilities. There is an emotional toll and psychological impact from fighting through situations that lead women to internalize the worry that they are not good enough or have more to prove to themselves and their peers in the workplace. They are plagued by the question of what they must do to be embraced as an exceptional colleague worthy of the position they hold and capable of rising in the organization.

I have been blessed to have my efforts and accomplishments recognized throughout the years with several awards and accolades, including the following:

- The Georgia Titan 100, 2024 – Presented by Wipfli LLP. Recognizes the state's top 100 CEOs and C-Suite executives
- Top 101 Influencers, 2024 – Inspiring Workplaces
- 2024 Women Empower & Women Excel Award – Georgia State University
- 50 Inspirational Women Leaders in Atlanta, 2024 – Briefcase Coach
- Top 100 Women in Sports, 2021, 2023 – Presented by Sports Inclusion Conference
- Top 100 HR Professional Award, 2021, 2022, 2023 – Presented by OnCon
- Icon. Identified as being an exceptional HR resources professional to the HR community
- 100 Women of Influence, 2020, 2021, 2022, 2023 – Presented by Atlanta Business League
- Distinguished Alumni Award, 2020 – University of Georgia-Athens, College of Family and Consumer Sciences
- Women of Excellence, 2018 – Atlanta Tribune
- The Pegasus Award for Excellence in Human Resources nomination, 2013 – Society for Human Resource Management, Atlanta Chapter

Early in my career, I attempted to tackle the storm of such negativity on my own. I internalized the anguish but quickly found that approach was ineffective in controlling the intense emotions. I suffered with migraines and panic attacks that varied in severity, with one requiring a visit to the emergency room. The only person in the organization who knew the extent of my turmoil at that time was my personal assistant, who graciously drove me to the hospital. I developed manageable paranoia and felt some odd sense of solace when I realized other women experienced imposter syndrome regularly as well. They had the same harmful drain on their physical and mental health as they struggled to overcome unavoidable self-doubt and self-deprecation that inevitably resulted in depression.

My tendency to reflect and analyze led me to realize that the imposter syndrome feelings and accompanying negative side effects that I experienced kicked into high gear most often when I felt attacked by other women. The unfortunate and unproductive ways in which females all too often work against each other is another tangential aspect to the problem of empowering women in Corporate America. There is the fight to be employed, the fight to be promoted, the fight to gain respect that is readily handed to men, the fight to be treated equitably compared to male colleagues, and then the additional fight that exists when females think the best strategy for them to get ahead is to attack the lady in the adjacent office.

I know this behavior is rampant because unfortunately, females have been my nemesis throughout my career and within my graduate school experience. Remember the chair of my doctoral committee whose words and actions made me question if I could in fact complete my Ph.D. Recall the female supervisor who as my peer moved me to a cubicle and made it clear she knew I lacked leadership abilities. I know I will never forget the lady who wrote the anonymous letter to announce within the company my presumed failures both as a manager and a person in an attempt to malign my name. I am convinced her ultimate goal was to have me fired. The woman who, after I took on the role as her supervisor, pretended to be my friend as a means to silence her team members and cover her own inadequacies is yet another example of the headaches and heartaches that have been launched my direction by a female.

Why is it that women who are all struggling to make the cement above them crumble do not join hands to achieve professional success as a powerful and united force? Why introduce additional pressure by opting to be rivals when each one is starting at a deficit with regard to opportunity and equity? Such behavior does not improve the bleak employment situation for women overall. It certainly does not advance either the perpetrator or the victim but rather fuels stereotypes about women in the workplace, reinforcing the barriers that keep them from thriving and rising in Corporate America.

I suggest that the answer lies in the thinking that too many women embrace, especially Black women, which is that no more than one within the cohort can advance. They become convinced that there is room at the top for only a single victor, and they are going to make sure it is not the other person who reaches the pinnacle. They may actually succeed in suppressing their female peers and seize the prized title, but they will not be able to sustain the position because eventually their destructive actions while clawing to the executive spot will be revealed. One exception I have found to this mindset is older women, who throughout my career have been genuinely supportive and encouraging, versus younger women who consistently adopt more of a warrior mentality.

With such deep-seated and misguided thinking, it is not surprising that women struggle to create trusting relationships at the office. Remember that the numbers show there is a small cohort of women in Corporate America to begin with, so there is a huge sense of disappointment when those who are present become an adversary instead of a confidante. Doubt as to if a colleague is sincere in reaching out or looking for a weakness to eventually attack is always present because too many women are convinced a show of support gives away their competitive advantage. A nurturing sense of camaraderie consequently rarely exists among women in the office, which I argue contributes further to their failure to advance. In all candor, I confess to having stifled meaningful relationships that would perhaps have blossomed into lifelong connections because I was unable to build trust with an individual.

Trust is tough because there is an abundance of evidence that yesterday's mean girls have become today's female bullies throughout Corporate America. Their toxic behavior exacerbates isolation and makes it difficult to regain confidence to keep climbing. Insulting and demeaning situations that stem from the behavior of men is also obviously unpleasant, however, I find it less surprising because the stereotypes that position women as being universally inferior make such moments expected if not inevitable.

I frankly anticipate more and better from those of my own gender and yet, I know from what I have endured as well as myriad examples shared by my mentors, friends, and a network of colleagues that it is not an exaggeration to say there are instances where women are truly vicious toward their female coworkers. The negative and often persistent behavior causes the imposter syndrome to resurface, along with the accompanying physical and mental ailments.

Finding the appropriate response when attacked is always a challenge, especially for women like me who do not have a passive-aggressive bone in their body and much prefer a partnership to being plunged into constant conflict. I embrace a strategy developed by relying on the wisdom of trusted mentors who advised me to stop worrying about how others perceived me or my work. I learned the value of tuning out the noise, which is an active decision I still practice, and I adopted the mantra that the opinion of others is none of my business.

I also began to understand the value of using my voice along with the wisdom of knowing what to address when and in what manner. I made the conscious decision to stop wasting my words when being attacked by a female coworker and resist the immediate impulse to lash out in a full-on confrontation. Doing so is a step toward engaging in self-sabotage that I guarantee will never eliminate the self-doubt that hits when aggressions persist or insults are hurled but could most definitely tarnish your professional brand.

I also have stopped wasting my energy trying to comprehend the reason for the other person's actions, which I realize could stem from insecurity, jealousy, or simply their hostile nature. Honestly, I no longer believe the motive is important but rather choose to focus on a deliberate and strategic reaction to the behavior, which may require I take the necessary time to reflect on what happened and evaluate options before determining an appropriate rebuttal. Pausing keeps me from responding in a like manner, which is not only counterproductive but portrays me as having the same negative traits as my offender.

I always consider how others will view me based on the actions I take, which is why I opt for extending professional courtesy, often while clarifying that trust has been destroyed. Taking this stance does not equate to inaction but rather ensures against engaging in reactionary behavior that gives the attacker the power. I choose to disengage and find resolution when I am less emotional and have settled on the best positive plan that allows all individuals involved to go forward. This strategic approach guarantees that I never allow anyone to take me to a place where I do not want to be.

To put it bluntly, I am not going to empower anyone to drag me into the gutter just because that is where she chooses to exist. I will maintain my character and continue to exhibit my true self, no matter how tiring it becomes to function at a higher level. My ultimate goal is to never walk away with regret for what I said or did regardless of what transpired against me. An even greater priority now that I work from the C-Suite is to be a leader in seeking resolution to the obstacles females encounter in the workforce and may even create based on their behavior.

The first crucial step in bringing positive change is to speak loudly and openly about the obvious. As reinforced by the statistics, the inability of women to rise in force in Corporate America is not a new phenomenon or a secret just being revealed. It is instead a proverbial disease that few want to admit exists or take action to eliminate. As television personality Dr. Phil McGraw preaches, we cannot change what we do not acknowledge.

It is also imperative for the problem to be viewed with a broad lens so that it is no longer seen as a woman's issue. Gender and race are a phenomenon that organizations are going to have to contend with as long as they do business and hire employees. Any time either gender or race are used to limit access and curb success, there is a negative impact felt by all. Any time voices are silenced either by exclusion or intimidation, there is a loss of potential that again impacts everyone. Ultimately, the empowerment of women to join the ranks of corporate leadership—and especially Black women—transcends any individual's achievement. It is a shared imperative for organizations and society at large. By acknowledging and addressing the systemic barriers that persist, we move closer to realizing a future where all individuals— regardless of race or gender—can ascend to positions of power and influence.

I passionately believe that each person must become engaged and insist on change in order for there to be significant progress. I especially challenge men to take up the mantle and join the effort to empower women in the workplace. Given men are predominantly today's executive leaders, they are positioned to voice support for women and push for initiatives that will result in a clear path forward for them within Corporate America. Men must actively engage in advocating, sponsoring, and mentoring while networking at an elevated and intentional level so that they make it their goal to open doors of opportunity for women to prove themselves and excel. Women must do likewise by planting seeds of change for the next generation and paying it forward as role models invested in sharing their wisdom with the young ladies still struggling to persevere and find their place as they build their careers.

The issues surrounding women in Corporate America are undoubtedly complex and so ingrained that it is not likely change will rapidly evolve. Believe me, I recognize that this reality can be discouraging and drain the motivation to engage in shifting the paradigm. When I succumb to such thoughts that make it seem defeat is inevitable and my efforts are in vain, I revisit the concept of The Butterfly Effect. As explained by The Decision Lab, an applied research and innovation firm, The Butterfly Effect "rests on the notion that the world is deeply interconnected, such that one small occurrence can influence a much larger complex system. The effect is named after an allegory for chaos theory. It evokes the idea that a small butterfly flapping its wings could, hypothetically, cause a typhoon."

The theory dates back centuries as it was put forth by Benjamin Franklin, who penned a proverb that conveys the power of one small act or, conversely, what happens when there is an oversight that appears to be inconsequential. Let his words be a rallying cry for us to unite. When we do, there will be positive change that will empower women and in turn, elevate Corporate America.

For the want of a nail, the shoe was lost.
For the want of a shoe, the horse was lost.
For the want of a horse, the rider was lost.
For the want of a rider, the battle was lost.
For the want of a battle, the kingdom was lost.
And all for the want of a horseshoe nail.

LESSONS LEARNED

There is a level of irony in the fact I feel I must address the way Corporate America is failing to enrich and empower women given I am a Black female executive who spearheads and implements people capital initiatives. I am painfully aware that Human Resources is supposed to be the conscience of the company or organization. I firmly believe that HR is the division charged with supporting individuals, leaders, and teams to be and do better. The mission of every HR manager at any level is to make sure every person has opportunities to excel, is seen for their value and potential, and has a voice that is heard.

Failure to demand and execute a plan to empower females so that they are valued as members of top executive teams in corporations across the country will result in perpetuation of the current paradigm, which in turn guarantees the continual crippling of individuals as well as companies.

Contemplating both realities leaves me angered, baffled, and increasingly motivated to courageously use my voice. I will continue to speak loudly and frequently about the need to redefine the role of women in Corporate America, as well as remove obstacles that are in essence barricades on their professional path.

We as a nation have not succeeded in reaching that goal with regard to the recruitment, retention, compensation, and promotion of women. We have also failed to address the way in which women often ostracize each other and add barriers intentionally set to ensure others do not rise to prominence and take the coveted executive suite seat. The disdain for this lack of camaraderie was perhaps best voiced by former Secretary of State Madeleine Albright. She stated in a keynote address to women of the WNBA that "there is a special place in hell for women who don't help other women."

The crippling abusive cycle can be broken if we learn the valuable lesson of building community. Let me repeat the need to create your own tribe, a circle of individuals you trust to not only provide valuable feedback and advice but create a safe place to retreat. They will renew your confidence as they listen to your pain and affirm your abilities. If you do not yet have such a support system in place, start building it today. Find the souls who will stand shoulder-to-shoulder with you and keep you upright when the attacks come and the doubts run rampant. Find the people who will be your strength and voice of truth as you battle imposter syndrome, which unfortunately will persist throughout your career. I view my own battle against it as similar to an alcoholic who pushes forward every day determined to defeat a lurking demon.

When you are under attack, do not succumb to the behavior of your nemesis, but rather stay true to who you are and your brand. I consistently remind myself of the words former First Lady Michelle Obama used in her 2016 Democratic National Convention speech when addressing how to handle bullies: "When they go low, we go high." Take the professional high road that empowers you to handle the situation without losing your dignity or tarnishing your reputation. I believe it is also critically important to stop wasting energy on trying to understand the motive behind the person's behavior. Heed the wisdom shared by American author Maya Angelou: "When someone shows you who they are, believe them the first time." Accept that your attacker is not going to change and a strained professional relationship may be all that is feasible, then tune out their negativity in order to focus on taking your next step upward.

Part of your professional plan must be to mentor, which is yet another means for painting a brighter picture for women in Corporate America. The women who remain in junior roles need your wisdom, encouragement, and honesty about what they will encounter as they mature in their careers. They need to know how to handle the hardships. When today's leaders unite to support, sponsor, and mentor those behind, a paradigm shift will occur because a professional environment where iron sharpens iron will begin to exist for females who will inevitably be elevated as a result.

Obstacles will never be replaced with opportunities, however, until there is equally strong unity in speaking out against what is occurring and demanding change. Let me repeat that the problems crippling Corporate America are not a woman's issue or a Black woman's issue. They are an albatross for every person and for every corporate entity. Solutions need to be openly discussed, strategies for improvement need to be debated, and a determination to improve needs to be embraced. Men must be actively engaged in this call to action, as they currently hold a position of power.

I consider the effort that will be required to change the paradigm for women in Corporate America to be as intense and significant as the fight for civil rights was in this country during the 1950s and 1960s. An equally loud cry for change is needed to create a corporate culture where there is an embraced equality that results in individuals arriving and thriving regardless of gender. We need a movement. Why? Because the habitual practice of overlooking or purposefully excluding women from the ranks of corporate leadership and relegating those who are hired to lesser status when comparing perks and pay will continue to persist until and unless all individuals regardless of race or gender unite to unlock doors of opportunity for women.

8

WEATHERING THE CHALLENGES
OF A NEW NORMAL

F ORECASTERS HAVE A POTENTIALLY HIGH-RISK LIVELIHOOD AS THEY attempt to provide predictions and warnings based on information they gather and interpret. In some instances, lives depend on their ability to complete an analysis quickly and accurately. This is especially true for meteorologists responsible for issuing alerts as radar shows dangerous weather rapidly enveloping a region. Families hurry to the safe zone of a basement as sirens blare because a tornado is about to touch down, just as coastal residents know based on the explanation of scientific calculations when it is time to evacuate in advance of a strengthening hurricane.

There are also those who focus on economic forecasts, working to offer advance notice about an accelerating rate of inflation, an impending downturn in consumer spending, the fluctuating strength of Wall Street, or business trends that are looming on the horizon. While the impact of these predictions is rarely life-threatening, knowing that such change is anticipated can ease the level of shock felt at the check-out line of the grocery store as prices surge, empower a CEO to prepare for a necessary budgetary shift, or change the decisions of shareholders who invest in the stock market with the hope of a strong return.

Despite the intensity and level of due diligence forecasters exert in anticipating what lies ahead, there are inevitably unforeseen circumstances or phenomena that initially create some degree of chaos that is typically followed by change. This is true in nature as well as Corporate America, which is where I and my HR colleagues have in recent years weathered some significant storms that have reconfigured the profession. Events that have shifted the paradigm of how Human Resources functions within an organization include social unrest and a racial reckoning ignited by the murder of George Floyd at the hands of police officers, as well as the upheaval created as a deadly pandemic swept across the globe into the U.S.

Suddenly HR professionals were elevated in the eyes of the CEO and members of the leadership team who were seeking answers to complex issues that rocked the workplace. Respect for the expertise and insights of those in Human Resources rose exponentially and as a result, the contributions of the unit shifted from primarily transactional to strategic. This in turn translated into much higher expectations for what the CHRO could deliver in terms of solutions that were often crucial for an organization's long-term success. There was an enormous sense of satisfaction tied to the awakening of what HR could do and should be as a function within a company, and simultaneously an intensified level of pressure to perform as it became obvious the traditional way of doing the job was rapidly becoming archaic and far from adequate.

To grasp the significance of what has transpired in HR requires an understanding of how the field has been perceived since the position of employment clerks was created early in the 20th century versus how the profession is now positioned. The mission, purpose, contributions, and responsibilities tied to Human Resources have shifted significantly in Corporate America the past 75 years, and certainly since I began my career nearly three decades ago.

In my early years, those individuals working in the field that initially relied predominantly on female employees were frequently viewed so disparagingly that they were sadly referenced on occasion as "lunch whores." Others used the word "lepers" to describe the HR team, which was also deemed to be the fun crew that did the light work because they were the employees who chose the supposedly softer field within Corporate America's structure.

Indeed, HR was "once considered a sleepy backwater of the C-Suite, a lesser-than role akin to a paper-pushing hall monitor," observed Paige McGlauflin in an article she authored for *Fortune* magazine in 2024. She noted that "CHROs weren't always in the limelight. HR leaders have historically been some of the lowest-paid executives, excluded from the C-Suite level and relegated to focus on nonstrategic issues like payroll, hirings, firings, and benefits."

My experiences confirm these statements were in fact the reality for far too long and unfortunately, the reduced role still persists as the norm in some sectors. In those instances, the

HR unit as a whole is typically seen as the office that demands hoops be jumped through in order to bring on board a desired employee or dismiss the one who needs to leave the organization. Once the hiring and firing is completed, there does not seem to be much appreciation for anyone assigned to an HR function and even less interest in understanding the vital work being done on behalf of the organization.

I learned as I tackled HR leadership roles in different industries just how broad the spectrum is with regard to the way Human Resources is viewed and valued. Recall that I have led in divergent industries ranging from professional services, restaurant retail, nonprofits, financial services and media conglomerates. I am fortunate to have experienced work environments where the HR office was already seen as strategic and vital in the partnership of both designing the organization's structure and contributing to its overall success long before my arrival. I have also survived employment situations where I felt every day was a fight to prove the importance of what Human Resources can provide as a company competes to become and remain stellar in providing a product or meeting a need.

That struggle for a stronger voice and opportunity to contribute while seated at the executive table where strategy is discussed and long-range plans are developed eased as protests escalated in the wake of Floyd's murder on May 25, 2020. A 46-year-old Black man detained under suspicion of using a counterfeit bill in making a purchase, Floyd was at the mercy of four white police officers who responded to a store clerk's call in Minneapolis, Minnesota. One of the officers, Derek Chauvin, knelt on Floyd's neck with such force and for so long that he died from a lack of oxygen. The officers were fired and convicted while the city awarded Floyd's family $27 million in a wrongful death lawsuit. As calls for justice

Evidence that Corporate America took notice of the murder of George Floyd and responded by embracing initiatives to spark change in the workplace was documented through a survey completed by the HR Policy Association in the spring of 2021. Nearly 400 HR leaders representing 11 million employees responded to questions regarding how their approach to their job changed after the tragic death.

- 85% of the respondents said inclusion activities increased, as did their involvement in the C-Suite

- 70% started or enhanced unconscious bias training

- 57% moved to disaggregate workforce data to gain a better sense of employee demographics

- 50% sought to hire from educational institutions with strong minority talent

- Other changes included the introduction of listening sessions, anonymized resumes, community partnerships, and a redesign of incentive metrics based on diversity

and societal change continued to escalate in communities across the country, Corporate America was left to contemplate the appropriate response to the core issue of human rights.

"Organizations started using words like 'structural racism' and 'racial injustice' or 'social injustice,' words they were not using before," according to Kerrien Suarez, executive director of Equity in the Center, which is a nonprofit devoted to building a race equity culture and based in Washington, D.C. "That shift in language is notable," Suarez said in the *Fortune* article, "and it resulted in a significant amount of unrest within companies because they were using language that people on their board might not be comfortable with."

The level of angst escalated within Corporate America as the Black Lives Matter movement surged. CEOs turned to HR professionals for guidance in implementing DEI initiatives intended to become sustained processes with the goal of elevating people of color to positions of leadership. Diversity committees became common, with members charged to explore sustainable change in the areas of racial justice and diversity.

Results varied but included such actions as tying the compensation of a company's top leadership team to progress made on DEI objectives or the implementation of practices to recruit and retain diverse employees. In some instances, diversity recruiters were added to HR teams as the emphasis within companies expanded to include focusing on creating a race equity culture. In many cases, DEI councils were created to work on programming for staff to incorporate inclusion and create a welcoming environment.

I was in my executive role when Floyd was murdered, which at the time was not the only storm brewing. The same year, COVID-19 changed everyone's daily life and put workplaces into a tailspin. There was suddenly confusion, if not panic, surrounding how individuals could continue in their jobs while remaining safe from the virus that was killing thousands daily and ultimately resulted in the death of more than one million in the U.S. alone.

Suddenly, HR professionals who had been seeking a seat at the executive table *became* the table as leaders from all sectors of the company had urgent employee questions that had to be answered immediately. CEOs and members of their team were a captive audience waiting for guidance and direction on how to handle myriad complicated topics that included policies regarding testing requirements and provisions, stipulations for the wearing of masks and the plan for enforcement, responses to rapidly changing federal or state guidelines, parameters for working from home, as well as measuring productivity following the closure of offices. The fact schools shut down as well created the problem of how to accommodate employees who were suddenly needed by their young children as they were forced to learn from a distance because they too were sent home.

The issues varied in terms of complexity depending on the industry and type of work assigned, with emergency services and healthcare employees facing the most difficult dilemmas. Unique problems existed for those of us in the arena of professional sports as well, given a percentage of the seasonal payroll covers game-day staff who were left without an income when the schedule was put on hold and even after play eventually resumed but without anyone in attendance. There was the issue of every refrigerator in Truist Park having been stocked in preparation for hungry fans coming out to the ballpark. Thankfully, both of those headaches were eased when we created a plan for the temporary staff to help with the distribution of the food, which is just one example of how strategic thinking was put into play when the season stalled.

The silver lining to that ominous cloud created by the pandemic? HR professionals across the country became recognized as capable of providing insight and guidance to navigate churning and uncharted waters. As a result, the relationship between the CHRO and CEO was developed or strengthened in countless corporations nationwide, opening the door for Human Resources professionals to have a stronger voice going forward. The fact that HR teams from coast to coast responded with the stamina and savvy of superheroes during the George Floyd travesty and pandemic panic raised the level of credibility and attention given to the field overall.

It also put a spotlight on how those who manage people capital function differently in what I refer to as times of war and peace. We have to be able to make the right decisions quickly and be comfortable pivoting on a daily if not hourly basis when a crisis makes all norms disappear. Those who prove themselves in the quiet season excel when battles surface because they have already gained the ear, confidence, and respect of leadership by providing relevant knowledge on an ongoing basis. I would argue the temporary calm after any storm is the ideal time for those of us in HR leadership roles to further embrace and advance the strategic thinking perspective that is crucial to the health, happiness, and productivity of employees going forward.

I am certain and grateful that the education I completed, added to the experiences I gained at each place of employment throughout my career, equipped me to be an effective leader in both times of calm and chaos. There were few if any specific HR academic programs offered within higher education when I was at the start of my career, which is why I opted to study for my MBA degree as preparation for entering the field. I consequently brought to every employer I partnered with a business acumen perspective that was initially developed through my graduate education and strengthened as a result of my unique resume. By definition, this approach combines knowledge with experience to develop problem-solving skills that are used to create action plans executed with confidence. Specifically, I always engage from a strategic position that involves understanding and managing the transactional needs tied to HR but advances initiatives that go far beyond the basics to empower individuals and ultimately enrich the company. It is for that reason that I explain my work is in people capital versus HR. The difference is more than semantics, as was clearly and quickly made apparent during the two crises discussed. Both resulted in the emergence of the new normal for those who hold executive positions within Human Resources.

In this reimagined role, HR leaders must be knowledgeable, credible, and aware. They must also be prepared to succeed in an expanded role that will rely heavily on analytics, fluidity, and agility.

Failing to adjust to the elevated expectations after recognizing the paradigm shift that has occurred within Human Resources would be equivalent to realizing a turn in the weather has been forecasted and doing nothing to prepare for the impending storm. Understanding the philosophical approach is consequently merely the first step for HR leaders who must learn how to bridge the divide between changing theory and increasingly complicated practice. I do so by consistently emphasizing the need for a strategic action plan, which I begin to work on immediately in any new position by making an organizational scan my first task. This obviously requires thoroughly comprehending the CEO's directives and priorities. From there the work entails conducting one-on-one interviews with each HR professional I am leading to learn what is going well, the challenges that exist, and the aspirations for improved performance either as individuals or a unit. I also meet with the team as a whole to understand from my direct reports the intersections, redundancies, and frustrations tied to the processes in place.

I am frequently invited to present at professional and academic events where I am asked to speak on the concept of the "new normal" for HR leaders. New normal is a phrase used in reference to a mode of operation that exists following a crisis, such as COVID-19, which definitely elevated the level of respect for and appreciation of HR teams in Corporate America across the country. I advocate that the CHRO must be a change leader, an operational leader, and an executive coach to continue functioning at the strategic level.

- Be the chief of scenario planning and transformation, which involves disrupting and resetting
- Be the chief of inclusion
- Excel as a chief player and coach

These interactions allow me to begin building relationships while gaining knowledge needed to evaluate the inner workings and strength of the organization's framework. It is essential that employees understand my intent is to partner with them and provide support versus becoming a negative force that inquires with the intent of finding fault. Recall my servant leadership approach, which I want to convey to all my direct reports from my first day in the executive role. In addition to building a rapport with my team, these initial interactions provide insight into the transactional functions of the HR work being done, specifically how well such basics as hiring, onboarding, firing, and handling of the payroll are executed. It is imperative to know the strength of the foundation upon which all the advanced and strategic initiatives will be built.

I also investigate beyond the walls of the HR office, scheduling conversations with each member of the executive leadership team to learn what is transpiring across the company in an effort to understand the successes, roadblocks, and red flags that exist on the whole. This also continues the effort to build relationships and often results in finding a top-level ally to partner with when pushing for change that may not initially be deemed desirable by some cohorts within the firm. A physical visit to the building offices occupied by individuals working in other areas of expertise within the company is imperative so I have a deeper sense of the employee structure than can be acquired by studying an organizational flowchart. I gather all of these pieces required to complete the scan within a maximum of 90 days so that I have the information needed to begin creating an action plan that encompasses immediate, mid-range, and long-term goals.

The specifics of the plan depend on the organization, however, I quickly learned the wisdom of beginning with praise for all that is being done well when reporting on the current condition before addressing the first critical need that is crippling the organization, such as a staffing shortage. I then pick the low-hanging fruit when suggesting changes be made. By this I mean starting with transitions that are not considered threatening or dramatic so that there is more likely to be acceptance by the team or across the company. An example would be aligning the talents of existing employees with tasks or shifting functions to improve efficiency.

I implemented that exact decision when working for the nonprofit, where I discovered from the organizational scan that the agency would be better served if payroll services moved from Human Resources to the finance and accounting office. Within that same agency, I discovered gaps in the HR team's cohesiveness and communication in part because the roles and responsibilities of each employee were not clearly defined. This was yet another easy fix and win that improved the satisfaction of frustrated individuals while bolstering the overall function of the organization.

The goal is to continue building toward a more difficult agenda while addressing complex issues that fall into the strategic category such as DEI initiatives, programs to address employee mental and physical health, and controversial topics tied to the moment in time. The debate still ongoing across the country about how to bring employees back into the office after they worked from home during the pandemic and do so without a wave of resignations or the loss of key talent is an example of how a current event can dictate what needs to be tackled next when drafting a strategic plan. The split between those who advocate for working from home versus others who are adamant that everyone must be seated at their office desk to remain employed is just one of many complicated issues that linger following the COVID-19 surge and are still being addressed with mixed results. Individuals want more flexibility in their lives, which means Corporate America must find a way to remain flexible without compromising the quality of the product being produced or service provided.

Once in place, the strategic plan created in conjunction with the company's CEO, executives, and my HR team is never considered complete because the process of gathering information and evaluating is a never-ending cycle. Employee satisfaction surveys will indicate areas where further improvement is needed, just as exit interviews with individuals who are leaving the organization always shine a light on what issues must still be addressed. The organization's objectives will evolve and expand, requiring revisions be made to reach goals not previously articulated.

There will always continue to be events across political, religious, legislative, and cultural arenas that force further reflection within organizations. Everything from the passage of a wage bill to advancing technology requires HR executives to adapt as they manage the endless cycle of recruiting and onboarding, developing and coaching employees, managing employee performance, and completing workforce planning all with the goal of moving the company upward and onward. That, of course, requires recruiting and onboarding the best employees, which results in the circular steps being repeated.

How to maintain the momentum and keep the elevated HR status in place is a key challenge going forward, as there is the danger of people capital and talent strategy once again being placed in the shadows of Corporate America. One way to avoid that pitfall is for CEOs to continue demanding more than transactional work from the Human Resources team, as

Further proof that the function of HR has expanded and shifted is provided through a listing of the top 10 HR priorities for organizations in 2024, which was compiled by McLean & Company. The HR consulting firm that focuses on research conducted a survey of nearly 1,400 business professionals to better understand what professionals in the field see as their 10 greatest challenges in the current year. Note that each entry is tied to a strategic goal.

1. Recruiting/Talent Acquisition
2. Providing a great employee experience
3. Controlling labor costs
4. Developing the organization's leaders
5. Supporting change
6. Enabling innovation
7. Fostering an environment of diversity, equity, and inclusion
8. Facilitating data-driven people decisions
9. Enabling learning and development
10. Rapidly moving internal employees to staff priorities

emphasized in McGlauflin's *Fortune* article. I am convinced that it is equally imperative for HR leaders to embrace their expanded role while working with fluidity and agility.

There must also be a commitment to continual learning as they devise ways to further enrich their organization. This will inevitably require becoming comfortable with analytics that are integral to innovative thinking about complex issues such as what traits will define the future workforce or where the budget can be trimmed today to realize cost savings tomorrow. Emerging technology will remain a constant element of change that will create continual challenges and further demand that every CHRO embrace the goal of being transformational.

Beyond the transition to automating transactions that range from direct deposit payroll to paperless employee applications, the growing use of Artificial Intelligence (AI) is a primary concern for HR executives. There is an anticipation that AI will be a positive tool used to expedite monotonous and time-consuming tasks so that attention and efforts can be shifted to the strategic work that only humans can accomplish. This hope was confirmed through a study completed by Workday Inc., a software vendor specializing in managing company workforces.

Workday surveyed 2,355 senior business executives in 2023 and found there is the expectation that AI will improve performance management tasks such as drafting employee reviews, skills management that includes identifying talent and emerging skills, and in the area of recruitment and onboarding through the review of applications and drafting of employment offers. Respondents also voiced concerns about implementing AI, noting there is the potential that its use could introduce a potential bias or errors while creating uncertainty about the level of security and privacy needed to protect personal employee information.

Worries about such anticipated challenges that are in clear view can be compounded for HR executives by anxiety that escalates with thoughts about all that is still unknown going forward. Further change is inevitable, just as I can announce with certainty that another crisis that originates either within Corporate America or from an outside force will at some point result in deeper reflection and additional revisions. It is certainly understandable that there will be moments of feeling overwhelmed during such tumultuous seasons. There will likewise be increased pressure and expectations placed on the CHRO as the workload shifts further still from being centered around the completion of transactional tasks to the delivery of strategic solutions for pressing problems.

I quickly realized when battling through a storm that it is never productive to succumb to the angst and enter into a panic or become the pessimist. I have instead learned to trust my skills and instinct as I keep my head on a swivel and my eyes on the end goal. I have proven in myriad difficult situations how gathering and dissecting data, partnering with the CEO and executive team to determine specific steps, and then leading my team to implement solutions is the best approach to reaching a positive outcome. I have learned to never forget all that I am capable of accomplishing as proven by my successes and the unique talents I bring to the table. That is, after all, what got me through the door to the C-Suite.

LESSONS LEARNED

The person most capable of remaining calm in the midst of a storm is likely to have already survived a similar experience. For example, while living in Kansas City, tornado season was a regular occurrence every year as the heat mounted during the summer. I learned to anticipate when the atmospheric conditions were right for a funnel cloud to form and was frankly more fascinated than frantic at the prospect of seeing one reach down from the sky. When I moved South and settled into a region more likely to be impacted by the remnants of a hurricane moving up from the Gulf of Mexico, I had to adjust to a different threat that felt far more intimidating until I became familiar with what such a storm would mean for my new neighborhood.

The same truth applies to any leader called upon to manage through a crisis, regardless of the profession. There is plenty of trepidation experienced by the executive who has never navigated through a complicated situation that occurs when chaos ensues and answers are far from obvious. I can say in all candor that my level of comfort when forced to manage through what felt like a nightmare evolved with experience to the point I now have innate knowledge of what to do when disaster strikes and the confidence to act without hesitation.

In my early years, I relied on those in my professional network as needed to provide the wisdom, insight, and calm needed for me to dissect what was transpiring so that I could become engaged and effective in problem solving. Do not hesitate to reach out to your mentors or trusted colleagues when searching for guidance to get through a proverbial storm. There is wisdom in recognizing the need to tap into another person's expertise. Doing so is empowering and far preferred to floundering or failing. Lean into their experience and embrace the opportunity to learn.

Confidence also comes through preparation, which always begins with anticipation. Put in the time and effort required to stay relevant in your field, meaning you are always aware of what is transpiring in your industry. This is the equivalent of knowing the forecast. Take whatever action is necessary for you to have a comfort level with the topics that are trending or to acquire the skills that are becoming necessary to excel in your position. It is equally imperative that you remain focused on what issues are igniting across your region and the nation. Go a step further and become so familiar with your organization and its leadership that you can anticipate what initiatives will be embraced and what topics are likely to cause a heated debate or create divisiveness. This level of knowledge will prove invaluable when you are called upon to assist in resolving an issue that needs to be addressed immediately.

Patience is yet another virtue that will serve you well when leading during a season of change, be it within an organization or across a profession as occurred in the field of Human Resources. Recognize the danger of attempting to alter too much too quickly, which at best can result in a sense of fatigue among employees and more likely will spark rebellion. The best way to avoid this additional level of chaos is to know the appetite for change among your company's leadership team and employee base. I have witnessed on numerous occasions scenarios where individuals were more content to deal with the pain of keeping the dysfunctional status quo than enduring the level of discomfort that comes from adopting a new routine. It may require waiting for that moment when change is recognized as not just avoidable but desirable before ideas can be implemented.

Regardless of what challenges you face when dealing with a crisis or while responding to a significant paradigm shift in your field, never lose sight of the basics. Always make it a priority to deliver all that is expected at the transactional level, even if you transition to become a strategic player in your organization. Set expectations and goals so that your team delivers quality consistently. Train, encourage, and provide feedback to each of your direct reports so that you have a solid partnership built on respect and trust. This is the foundation you will need to weather every storm in your company because you will have developed a team that will listen to your voice and will follow your lead.

9

EMBRACING A GLOBAL PERSPECTIVE

P ERCEPTION IS CRUCIAL TO THE FORMATION OF OPINION AND IS critically important to our level of understanding, as it shapes how we interpret all that we experience. Perception and perspective are consequently intertwined, with the latter influencing our beliefs and fueling the thinking that informs our decisions. The ability to see and perceive accurately is inevitably diminished given we rarely have full context of a situation, which leads to conclusions that are flawed because they take into consideration only partial truth. This perpetual dilemma is clearly and succinctly conveyed in the story of the blind men who described an elephant based solely on their touch of the animal.

A Buddhist parable that dates back to five centuries before the birth of Christ, the tale explains each man's conclusion about the elephant based on what part of its body they examined using only their hands. The one who felt the side of the animal declared it to be a wall, while the man who took hold of the tusk was certain the elephant was like a spear. The third man's comparison was to a snake, as he had grabbed ahold of the trunk. A tree was the verdict of the one who wrapped his hands around a knee, which was far different from the conclusion of the man who touched the elephant's ear. He felt certain it compared most closely to a fan. The sixth in the group seized the elephant's tail and asserted with confidence that the animal was just like a rope.

It is interesting to note that the men were technically correct in their analysis given the comparison each provided because of his personal experience was valid. They described what they touched with an appropriate simile. Each could argue his point with conviction based on what part of the elephant was examined. They all also simultaneously fell far from the mark of providing an accurate description of an elephant because they literally lacked the vision needed to consider the whole creature and gain a comprehensive understanding. The tale consequently becomes a warning that we each must remain aware of the fact our knowledge base is always limited. Our perspective and certainly our worldview develop as a result of our unique family heritage, cultural experiences, and personal journey, including the opportunities we have had to interact with individuals who differ from ourselves. Each perspective is valid and worthy of consideration, just as each is limited and needs to be tested before being considered conclusive and complete.

I have embraced this thinking throughout my career and incorporate it into my management style, which you will recall is situational. I value the uniqueness of each person as I preach and practice the call to recruit and welcome to the organization and specifically to every team I manage individuals with varied beliefs, backgrounds, and worldviews. Their voice must be heard for corporations to remain competitive in a globally interconnected marketplace, which is one reason why I have enthusiastically seized the task of creating DEI programs and initiatives while serving in various positions within different organizations. And yet, it was not until I had the opportunity to delve deeper into the international aspect of Corporate America with an overseas assignment requiring I live outside the U.S. that I fully appreciated the level of myopic vision that is both a norm and a hindrance in organizations across the country.

Remember that I was promoted to the role of vice president for Human Resources within a media conglomerate in 2012. My responsibilities were wide-ranging and included leading the human capital initiatives for the company's Global Technology Operations Division. Within the unit were teams tied to areas of audience multi-platform technologies, global network operations, technology development and services, and systems technology and engineering. I was barely one year into this new position when the CHRO approached me with the idea of working from Hong Kong as the company underwent a major transition requiring a level of HR expertise and savvy that could not be delivered at a distance from my U.S. office.

My first reaction was shock, as I had not anticipated such an amazing assignment would ever be offered. I certainly did not expect such a heavy responsibility so early in my tenure as a vice president, even though I had joined the corporation four years earlier. The fact that I had gained experience working with companies outside the U.S. throughout my career was no doubt a factor in my being seen as capable of such a complex work assignment. I had previously overseen operations in Latin

American regions, including working to support chief financial officers across Argentina, and had successfully completed initiatives that were undertaken in London.

The surprise also stemmed from the fact I was unaware of the significant global change taking place within the company, which stemmed from the hire of a new president from Germany to head the international sector's operations. His strategy was to revamp the business model for the corporation's Asia-Pacific (APAC) region that includes Korea, Greater China, and South-East Asia. Specifically, the goal was to transition the home office and employee base from Hong Kong to another foreign country, India. This was an enormous undertaking considering the logistics that ranged from legal to facility to personnel issues compounded by the need to continue production despite the significant disruption caused by such a shift.

I would not be transparent if I failed to confess that I felt quite a bit of anxiety and trepidation mixed in with a sense of excitement and gratitude for having been chosen to shepherd an initiative so critical to the company's global success. My mixed emotions stemmed in part from the fact I had never before been immersed in the country while completing an international assignment. There was also the reality that I was single at the time following the draining divorce and mom to two sons who were then in their teens. I was being asked to live and work more than 8,000 miles from my children and my HR team, which I would continue to manage while taking on the Hong Kong duties.

As I contemplated the weighty decision that would radically impact my personal life and potentially fuel my professional aspirations, I once again turned to my tribe for advice and guidance. I began with a call to my father. When I asked the question of how I could manage such a huge upheaval in my daily life and care for my sons while doing such intense work halfway around the world, he replied with a question of his own. *How can you not say yes?!* My father saw the wisdom of tackling such a fascinating work challenge that would allow me to grow exponentially and be uniquely prepared to go forward toward the C-Suite. I am forever appreciative of how he and my mother rallied as part of my support system so that I could experience what I will forever consider to be a highlight of my career.

My assignment was to be in Hong Kong for one month, but I was instead steeped in the international work from May through November of 2013. The stress began immediately as I only had one week from the time I was told of the work to the date of my departure. I was consequently scrambling to make the necessary arrangements for my sons, who were 16 and 14 at the time. Thankfully, they were excited for me and expressed no qualms about adjusting to a temporarily altered routine. One reason for their comfort level was that I was adamant the disruption to their lives would be minimal. They were heavily engaged in activities that ranged from participating in school events to playing on traveling sports teams and enjoying increased time with friends. All of that continued because I arranged for them to remain in our house under the care of rotating caregivers, primarily my parents and their father, my ex-husband. I also relied on friends in my network to assist with handling tasks such as transportation when necessary.

My parents were a huge blessing, leaving their home in North Carolina without complaint to be a core part of my support system. My former spouse, however, purposefully presented every glitch as a crisis and did his best to spark in me recurring guilty feelings about being a horrible mother–those nagging doubts that every female with children has as she balances career goals with family responsibilities. Recall that he was vicious in his remarks while we went through the divorce process, making it clear he perceived me to be the negligent parent who valued my career above all else. My international assignment only added fuel to his argument that my job was more important than my children. In reality, I literally went the extra miles to remain present in the lives of my sons. I established a schedule of being overseas for two weeks and then home for seven days before departing once again. I looked forward to participating in their activities throughout the week I was back, even though I was physically exhausted from the near 20-hour flight and struggled to continually adapt to the 12-hour time difference.

The time change was one of the hardest adjustments I faced in terms of acclimating to living in Hong Kong. I was understandably concerned about all aspects of my personal transition given there was no window for scheduling any cultural immersion conversations or training because I only had seven days to prepare. Thankfully I did not have any language issues to overcome because Hong Kong had been under British rule from the 1800s until it reverted to Chinese sovereignty in 1997. The fact English is universally spoken made it exponentially easier to adjust to the city with a population of approximately 7.5 million that reminded me of New York City, but with significant steroids added.

Both cities are bustling 24 hours a day, are marked by impressive skyscrapers, boast an international citizenry, and have a thriving business sector that is multifaceted. Both are recognized as a global financial hub as well as a cultural mecca. I was delighted by the opportunity to become acclimated to the new and exciting environment as much as possible around the work demands. My knowledge of Hong Kong's history increased markedly, and I could see the ways in which it had developed

ExPat Living, a publication that informs individuals who live in another country for a period of time or permanently and are known as expatriates, provides fun facts about Hong Kong.

- Hong Kong means "fragrant harbor" in Chinese.

- There are more than 8,000 skyscrapers, with the tallest nearly one-third of a mile high.

- The city has the longest covered escalator, which runs for half a mile.

- Citizens have an entrepreneurial spirit and desire to make money. Hong Kong ranked 7th on a global list of billionaires released in 2020 and has 96 residents worth $1 billion or more.

- The majority of the population speaks Cantonese.

- Hong Kong's international airport has acreage equivalent to 20 soccer fields.

into a massive metropolitan area that is clearly a blend of both Chinese and Western influences. The mix is apparent in everything from fashion to cuisine. It was amazing to sample spectacular restaurants, stroll through endless stores—yes, I purchased shoes!—and even make time to explore Hong Kong Disneyland.

Such moments of relaxing down time were delightful because they were rare given the enormous workload that I and two male colleagues from the U.S. office faced. They were assigned to focus on the changing business management pieces tied to moving the headquarters to a different country, which was work they completed rather quickly. I was there to provide support and knowledge for the human capital initiatives and did so by partnering with the HR team already in place. The diverse group included individuals from Persia, Tokyo, Singapore, and of course, Hong Kong. They were all people of color, which quickly stood out as unique compared to what I had experienced through my years as a manager in Corporate America.

Coming in as a turnkey leader who was focused on facilitating the move with the understanding I would then be returning to the U.S. would have been much more difficult if not for the fact the staff in place was exceptional. They already had experience supporting the company's operation in APAC nations ranging from India and Thailand to Australia, so I inherited a group of proven professionals. They welcomed me and another female who was an attorney working as a consultant charged with oversight of contracts.

There was a level of trust established fairly quickly, no doubt because the group realized the need for a leader to take charge of the complicated mission. Preparing them for the scope of our task was my priority and the most difficult aspect of the assignment, as they had not previously experienced or facilitated such an overwhelming corporate change. I was able to explain what we were facing, what had to be done, how we would handle each task, and pledged to support each of them at every step.

I initially anticipated I would experience some level of anxiety as the person managing what was essentially shifting a decentralized business to one functioning under a much more centralized model and making the change happen smoothly despite crossing the border from one country to another. I was very aware that I had not lived or worked in either country and was still learning the cultural and business norms. I also clearly did not know the HR regulations of either nation as I began the work, which involved creating a curriculum for change management. And yet, I felt incredibly comfortable providing the knowledge needed for team members to do their job. I relied on my experience and resorted back to what I refer to as my systematic playbook as I made decisions at a fast pace while still managing my team in the states.

At the same time of the assignment in APAC, my U.S. team remained focused on all of the initiatives that were launched before my departure. I still maintained the meeting schedule with my employees I supervised in the states as if I wasn't on an assignment across the globe. This meant juggling my schedule to continue the one-on-one meetings and departmental sessions as if I was still seated in the building. The challenge of supporting and advancing the work of teams situated across the globe was increased markedly because of the time difference. I used my frequent flight time to focus on agendas for each of the teams I was leading.

I quickly realized that despite working on another continent in a culture that was truly foreign to me, many aspects of the tasks tied to Human Resources that had to be done remained remarkably similar. For example, one of the most difficult functions an HR supervisor handles is removing an employee. Whether firing a person because of poor job performance or explaining that a position is being eliminated and the paychecks will consequently end, it is never pleasant or easy to deliver such negative news. That moment can understandably shake a person to their core as they often begin to doubt their abilities and are overcome with worry about meeting every need for themselves and family members. It was my responsibility to ensure these conversations went as smoothly as possible when team members told employees they were either going to have to relocate to another country or lose their position with the company.

This scenario is just a sampling of the practical, and in some cases painful, work that needed to be done with the Hong Kong team. To prepare them for the tough talks they would have with employees, I explained that it is imperative to predict how the scenario will play out based on the individual's personality and their current circumstances. Remember that situational management is always essential. If, for example, it is known that one employee is nearing a retirement decision, the emphasis in the discussion needs to be focused on how benefits will transfer or how they will be distributed if the person decides against moving with the company. While I understand separation conversations are never comfortable, enjoyable, or easy, I was grateful that my years of experience allowed me to empower my Hong Kong team members to know how to diffuse the situation simply by how they approached the topic.

What I did not share with them was the tense moments I have experienced firsthand when the employee involved became enraged. Very early in my HR career while still working for Pizza Hut, I fired a woman who I expected would not respond well to the news. I was prepared for a potential outburst and asked that a risk management staff member join our conversation. That proved to be one of my best business decisions, as she grabbed scissors off my desk and attempted to come at me in full attack mode. My coworker intervened and protected me from harm. I have also had to summon security when a terminated employee began stalking me. The risks tied to such dangerous actions taken by a disgruntled former employee are increasingly a hazard to every HR executive across the United States, which is why it is imperative that caution remain a top priority.

Thankfully such extreme situations did not occur during the difficult conversations held with Hong Kong employees whose jobs were being shifted, no doubt in part because of the work culture that exists in the country. There is an obvious level of professionalism engrained in individuals as workers respect the hierarchy within an organization and strive to maintain a healthy work environment. According to NNRoad, which provides HR services in more than 50 countries, Hong Kong citizens are greatly influenced by Chinese values and Confucian principles "such as respect for authority, filial piety, and the importance of maintaining harmonious relationships play a significant role" in the country's work culture.

Employees also adhere to the concept of guanxi, which is "the practice of building and nurturing social networks and relationships," according to NNRoad. This commitment results in an office dynamic characterized by collaboration and trust. Protocols are known and followed so that there is unity in the workplace and tasks are completed through consensus. From punctuality to respect for authority and acceptance of the fact decisions are made from the top down, Hong Kong employees are focused on achieving results. There is an intense level of motivation and dedication that results in a workforce known for consistently high performance and a continuous desire to improve. The downside to such a level of commitment is that the employee base consists largely of workaholics who struggle to maintain a healthy balance in life.

As is true for every region, the people of Hong Kong have specific traits that characterize the workforce. NNRoad has identified some aspects that make the city's work culture vibrant.

- Strong sense of discipline and a results-oriented mindset

- Engrained sense of fairness, a commitment to transparency, and respect for contracts

- Foundation of trust, collaboration, and long-term partnerships

- Respect for authority and hierarchical structures, with adherence to protocols and deference to superiors

- Professionalism, punctuality, a strong work ethic, and an attention to detail

- Open exchange of ideas and adapting best practices from a global perspective

- Long working hours and intense competition

In addition to gaining an understanding of how the U.S. workforce compares to Hong Kong employees with regard to core characteristics, I gained enormous insight into the handling of Diversity, Equity, and Inclusion initiatives internationally. DEI has increasingly been of interest and importance to me in part because the urgency for creating and implementing policies that emphasize acceptance and opportunity for all has gradually become a more significant aspect of my HR responsibilities. In the United States, however, DEI is still primarily grounded in the thinking of racial bias and the need to embrace initiatives that expand opportunities for individuals of color.

Working in Hong Kong, I realized that the U.S. still perceives DEI efforts as a tool to primarily improve a person's situation, while the global perspective is much more broad and centers on the belief that society as a whole can and must be elevated. The view in that country leans more toward the idea that enhancing DEI policies bolsters the nation's level of competition and sustainable development. A study published by the Hong Kong Chartered Governance Institute examined the tendency to move beyond the narrow view of diversity that focuses on obvious traits such as gender, race, physical abilities, and age, and put the emphasis on using DEI policies to fuel and sustain competitive economic development by creating a harmonious society. Mutual understanding is imperative for DEI initiatives to be so embraced and become so effective that social problems are addressed and their resolution made a universal priority.

Gaining such knowledge of how fundamental elements of Corporate America are defined differently compared to organizations internationally and integrated into the workplace uniquely in other countries allowed me to develop a much broader perspective about all aspects of doing business in

The Hong Kong Chartered Governance Institute emphasizes that DEI values align with nine of the 17 Sustainable Development Goals established by the United Nations.

- Goal 1: End poverty in all its forms everywhere.

- Goal 4: Ensure inclusive and equitable quality education and promote lifelong learning opportunities for all.

- Goal 5: Achieve gender equality, and empower all women and girls.

- Goal 8: Promote sustained, inclusive and sustainable economic growth, full and productive employment and decent work for all.

- Goal 9: Build resilient infrastructure, promote inclusive and sustainable industrialization, and foster innovation.

- Goal 10: Reduce income inequality within and among countries.

- Goal 11: Make cities and human settlements inclusive, safe, resilient and sustainable.

- Goal 16: Promote peaceful and inclusive societies for sustainable development, provide access to justice for all, and build effective, accountable and inclusive institutions at all levels.

- Goal 17: Strengthen the means of implementation and revitalize global partnership for sustainable development.

the U.S., from organizational structure and leadership style to valuing the role of each individual. While I was absolutely committed to embracing differences prior to my Hong Kong assignment, I returned realizing that I had been constrained by my myopic thoughts that were rooted in my limited professional international experiences. Exposure to Hong Kong's culture and employee base gave me a new level of empathy, understanding, and compassion as an executive. I was more committed to using a broader lens when evaluating situations and making decisions. I was energized and empowered by new knowledge that led to an enriched perspective and resulted in a greater appreciation for how our country fits into the global map of commerce. You could say I went from touching one part of the elephant to seeing its total grandeur.

LESSONS LEARNED

There is no disputing we live in a world so interconnected that much of what transpires in our country is dependent on what is happening in nations around the globe. From financial markets to technological advances and the influx of goods through trade agreements, we are all impacted by what our international neighbors are pursuing and accomplishing. Corporate America is also experiencing significant change as a result of globalization, which is bringing more diversity to the workforce and greater expectations of executives who must be able to manage across borders. This reality means that those of us in leadership must be ready and able to apply our expertise far beyond our company's stateside headquarters or be left behind despite our previous success.

Harvard Business Review made this point bluntly by stating in the article "The new path to the C-Suite" that "the skills that help you climb to the top won't suffice once you get there." Specifically, it is imperative that executives become more astute so that they can lead with the necessary knowledge of how individuals from various cultures interact, as well as understand how to meet the needs of employees from other nationalities so that their potential is maximized. There is the secondary challenge of having the skills to either create or function within a personnel development system that can be transferred around the world. This is essential as the trend of U.S. companies to make cross-border acquisitions and expand into other nations is certainly going to continue and more likely escalate.

The best way to be prepared for these challenges and adapt to tasks that are becoming increasingly complicated because of international and cultural aspects is to tackle an overseas assignment. As intimidating as it may seem, I promise you that there is no better method for gaining the insight and perspective needed to position yourself in Corporate America as the employee who is ready, able, and eager to tackle issues made complex because of a global component. You will widen your perspective as you expand your knowledge base and experience growth as both a person and professional in ways that are not feasible when situated in your home environment.

I recognize that living and working overseas is often not an option, however, there are still ways to increase your international knowledge and cultural awareness. Make travel to other countries a priority so that you can explore how others live around the world. Such leisurely adventures will provide insights and exposure that will broaden your thinking. Learn a foreign language and take advantage of local opportunities to expand your horizons through such activities as hosting an international student. If you do have the chance to live or work outside the U.S., make it a priority to complete immersion training if offered and if not, seek ways to prepare for the transition. Be patient with yourself, as there will be frustrations and times of self-doubt as you adjust to a new normal. Embrace the painful moments as a sign that you are growing and pushing yourself to a higher level of thinking and understanding that will empower you and benefit your employer.

I realized that my international experience was a season of growth that I did not want to end when I returned to the U.S. I felt I had in many ways reinvented myself as a person and leader who was ready to continue tackling challenging initiatives that would allow me to exercise my new worldview and apply the knowledge I had gained. It was frankly a disappointment to be placed back in my previous role, which I no longer found to be as interesting or challenging. I was ready for a change and consequently left the company soon after my return. You may have a similar experience after completing an international assignment and find you are experiencing a level of discontent. Take that as a positive sign that you have advanced to the next level because you gained a competitive advantage that comes with global experience. You have literally gone the extra mile to gain additional skills along with increased confidence so that you are ready to climb to the next rung of the corporate ladder. You have been empowered to unlock your next professional door.

10

LEAVING A LEGACY

THERE IS A STARTLING DISCONNECT BETWEEN A RESUME AND AN obituary. The first is an attempt to impress by detailing an extensive skill set, presenting a stellar track record of workplace success over the span of years, explaining the relevance of unique experiences, and conveying both an eagerness and confidence in securing the next position forward on a professional path. The latter is an equally important summation of an individual but one created for the purpose of looking back over a life that ended too soon.

The criteria for what is considered crucial in defining a person's accomplishments and how they should be remembered shifts significantly. The list of family roles ranging from sibling to spouse, parent, and beyond are highlighted instead of job titles. And while the career path is typically mentioned, the goal of an obituary is to emphasize character traits and selfless actions that exemplify how the loved one impacted others through word, deed, and example versus heap praise for completed work initiatives.

What I find most intriguing about both the resume and obituary is that every individual is ultimately in charge of how each will read. Decisions made about what to study, which field to pursue, where to work, and how to advance all shape the resume. Likewise, the priorities we set, attitudes we demonstrate, moral code we embrace, families we create, and the ways in which we invest in others all dictate the legacy that we leave. Ideally, the expertise and wisdom we acquire that are reflected on the resume become the tools we use to empower others and elevate our community through the purposeful use of our time and talents.

I learned long before launching my career that this approach to life brings a sense of accomplishment and fulfillment that matches, if not exceeds, the thrill tied to any personal or professional triumph. This truth was a mantra preached by my parents and grandparents, all of whom instilled in me during my childhood the perspective that helping others was a mandate instead of an option. As soon as I was physically able, I was included in family efforts to support others because we were not just richly blessed but also called to be a blessing. I should clarify that by any standard of measure, we were not a wealthy household. But as my father made clear, we had all of our needs met from a roof over our heads to clothes on our back and food on the table. That made us fortunate. We had been given much so in return, much was required of us to support others less fortunate.

I learned to put this into practice as a child when, for example, my parents typically adopted a family each holiday season. We were responsible for shopping to find gifts that matched the children's requests and provided a dinner. I was taken to shop for a toy or piece of clothing that was then donated to the family we were supporting anonymously. Rather than feel a sense of being cheated, I looked forward to the annual excursion to the store and did my best to find the perfect item that I felt certain would bring a smile to the face of another child I would never meet. I was excited to be actively included in a family tradition of giving and serving that was in place long before my birth.

My grandparents were part of a farming community that thrived through mutual support, be it helping others with planting, preparing meals for a family experiencing tough times, or going to a neighbor's property to partner in picking cotton. While my father was still a graduate student in the state of Washington, he and my mother chose to serve others by becoming actively involved in the National Urban League. An historic civil rights organization that dates back to 1910, the National Urban League relies on local volunteers to work for social justice, economic empowerment, and equality for underserved individuals, including African Americans. Education, job training, assistance with housing, and overall community development are just some of what is provided through the organization's outreach.

His personal pledge to provide support for those struggling in the community continued throughout his life and became a core aspect of my parents' marriage. From my earliest memories as a child in Kansas City, I recall witnessing a commitment to always offer aid without hesitation. We did just that so often that I grew to realize the trait of giving was intertwined in my family's DNA. We joined with members of our church congregation or individuals from community organizations to participate in food drives, clothing distribution, and work projects. I eagerly

My involvement in volunteer work has grown exponentially as I have risen in my profession and simultaneously expanded my network. With each new position comes additional opportunities to serve. And with each volunteer position accepted, more invitations to join other organizations and initiatives quickly follow. I count it a responsibility and a blessing to give back, which is why I have gladly invested my time and expertise in various ways throughout my career. The following is a sampling of my involvement as a volunteer over the past two decades.

- Alpha Kappa Alpha Inc. – Active member since 2019
- The Destiny Fund – 2006
- Pathbuilders – Actively involved as a mentee and mentor since 2002
- College of Family and Consumer Sciences at University of Georgia-Athens – Board Member, 2015-2018; President of Board, 2016-2017
- Society for Human Resource Management (SHRM)-Atlanta – Board Member 2017-2019; Board Development Chair 2018-2019
- TedXUGA speaker – March 2018
- International Women's Forum-Georgia (IWF) – Member since 2020; Board Member 2024
- Human Resource Leadership Forum (HRLF) – Member 2016-Present; Board Engagement Chair 2020-2021
- HR.com – Diversity, Equity, and Inclusion Advisory Board Member – 2021-2024

- Goodwill of North Georgia – Board Member and Compensation Chair 2020-2022; Board Member and Vice Chair 2022-2023
- American Heart Association Board Member – 2021-2023
- Reinhardt University Commencement Speaker – 2022
- 21st Century Leaders – Member and Board Effectiveness Chair 2020-2022; Board Chair 2022-Present
- Woodruff Arts Center – HR and Compensation Chair, Governess and Board of Trustees Member – 2020-Present
- University of Georgia-Athens – Alumni Association Board of Directors Member 2021-Present
- Atlanta Braves Foundation – 2022-Present
- Atlanta Rotary Club Member – 2022-Present
- Leadership Atlanta – Class of 2024

answered the call for volunteers when my high school was participating in an outreach initiative, and I happily partnered with my Alpha Kappa Alpha sorority sisters to complete service projects in the community.

It is consequently not surprising that from the start of my career, I actively searched for opportunities to step up and give back either through the corporation I had joined or by becoming engaged with local programs in place to meet a community need. Doing so fits with my work as an HR professional who is required to meet people where they are and support them as they seek to advance. The fact that giving back is part of my moral fiber is no doubt one reason I have become so passionate about the field. A determination to offer a helping hand in any way possible whenever feasible became even more integral to who I am at my core as I advanced in my career.

As noted in previous chapters, I have been blessed by those who saw my potential and acted on my behalf, willingly making an unexpected effort to open doors that led to exceptional opportunities. I have also encountered plenty of folks who made the conscious choice to be an obstacle as they did their best to divert my focus or destroy my potential. I chose long ago to join the team that is committed to making a positive difference, which is why I continually look for areas where I can use my voice to bring change. Doing so as a seasoned professional who volunteers her expertise is just one way I repay those who invested in me. In every instance, I have reaped enormous blessings in return for the effort.

Some of my earliest volunteer work as an adult was tied to my role as a single mom to two active boys who were involved in traveling sports and played on school teams. There were endless opportunities to step up and ensure all the needs for a successful season were met, from providing snacks for the players to participating in raising funds. Regardless of the win-loss record, the experience of supporting my children and their peers was as rewarding as it was at times exhausting, especially during the years of adding chauffeuring and chaperoning duties. And yet, I would not want to have missed a single minute of those long hours, as I strengthened the bond with my sons. Beyond enabling them to pursue a passion, I bolstered the family tradition of modeling for my children what it looks like to gladly step up and meet a need.

Mentoring was not surprisingly one of the first opportunities I became aware of within my career, as I was nurtured from the start by various professionals. They shared their insights and provided the encouragement I needed to gain the confidence and fortitude required to advance in the HR field. Realizing the benefit of such invaluable support, I was ready and eager to fill the same role as a mentor. Giving my time to build a personal relationship with someone younger or less experienced became a natural extension of my work, as my goal as an HR executive has always been to meet people where they are in their journey and empower them to go forward. I expanded my efforts from primarily an internal focus of guiding the members of my team to giving advice when sought out by acquaintances to eventually joining formal outreach programs.

Pathbuilders is one organization I have partnered with to connect with individuals who are seeking a professional mentor. Based in Atlanta, Pathbuilders has created mentoring programs across the country with the sole purpose of developing the talent of women as they prepare for leadership positions. There are more than 6,000 participants with ties to 500-plus companies, resulting in an enormous positive impact.

I appreciate the mission because as discussed in a previous chapter, there are too few women within Corporate America to provide the encouragement and guidance needed for more females to break the concrete ceiling. The ladies I have been fortunate to meet and mentor are typically mid-level managers who are frequently stymied by a sense of inadequacy and overwhelming defeat with no apparent ability to advance given they face endless challenges with minimal support. I can relate and more importantly, I can draw from my own experiences to provide solid advice for how they too can persevere.

I also enjoy connecting with college students, which is why I am grateful for the opportunity to volunteer through my alma mater, the University of Georgia in Athens. Earlier in my career, I served for three years on the alumni board for my specific College of Family and Consumer Sciences, with one year as president. Now I am a member of the alumni board that works on behalf of the entire university, which means more frequent visits to campus and participation at events where I am able to meet students still forming the foundation for their future career. I find they have a refreshing eagerness and a hunger to get started on their professional path. For many, their greatest weakness is the need to recognize and accept that they are starting a marathon versus a sprint, which means it is vital that they develop patience.

I typically mentor up to as many as 10 individuals at any given time, including those I meet with informally. Ascertaining where each person is on their journey and understanding their goals are essential first steps to helping them succeed. Gaining such insight requires investing time to listen intently as they explain the situations they are facing in the moment and share their aspirations. Those who expect me to provide a simple solution or detailed roadmap are disappointed because I believe problems are rectified and success achieved through self-discovery. I consequently focus on asking questions that require serious self-reflection and interject my insights with the intention of sparking their self-awareness. I am equally diligent in offering the encouragement and strength each person needs to find their voice.

The process can be draining, as there is obviously work involved when iron sharpens iron. There is simultaneously an invigoration as well because I am convinced that mentoring must be an act of reciprocity. I consider each partnership a symbiotic relationship as we learn from each other. I will never present myself as the person who has gained all the knowledge necessary and has nothing more to glean from others. I instead recognize that each person's unique experiences and perspective allow me to expand my thinking and find new ways to use my position and expertise to help build and sustain communities of support and encouragement.

I am consequently rejuvenated by the individuals I mentor, and I rejoice as they rise to reach their professional potential and goals. I am reminded of my own journey and filled anew with appreciation for those who supported me as I celebrate each success of someone I took under my wing. I am also grateful for the lifelong friendships that have resulted from mentoring opportunities, as I add the former student to my growing network of peers. For example, while I was working for the media conglomerate, I had the privilege of teaming with a young man who had the talent and desire to become a top-level HR executive. He put in the work and persisted to become the CHRO for a national television network and now sits in the headquarters located in New York City. We remain in contact and continue to support each other as we both advance in our careers.

In order to lead, I need to remain relevant in the profession that is constantly evolving. This requires a different level of volunteer work aimed specifically at organizations tied to the HR field. I have been actively involved with three that provide the training and networking sought by those who aspire to lead in Human Resources. SHRM, which stands for the Society for Human Resource Management, is a national organization dedicated to researching issues and advocating for innovation in the HR field. There are approximately 350,000 members in nearly 200 countries, making SHRM a powerful force for workplace change and a source of strength for those in the profession. I have served on the board of SHRM-Atlanta and chaired a committee to advance the local chapter's work of building up leaders through initiatives that range from conferences and mentoring programs to offering scholarships.

Similarly, I have served as an advisory board member on issues of Diversity, Equity, and Inclusion for HR.com, which boasts the largest network of HR professionals. An estimated 2 million individuals working in the field around the world are connected to this company's social networking platform that focuses on best practices with the goal of maximizing human potential in the workplace. The tools, advice, and training are invaluable to employees handling HR assignments at all levels. In addition, I served as the engagement chair on the board of Atlanta's Human Resource Leadership Forum (HRLF) chapter. Established as a forum for thought leaders in the industry to share innovative ideas and exceptional practices, HRLF provides growth opportunities for top executives.

Each of these professional networks creates an encouraging and supportive environment that increases knowledge, which in turn bolsters confidence. There is a refreshing affirmation experienced when meeting with your peers to discuss trends and brainstorm solutions to persistent problems. I often wonder how my earlier career struggles would have been lessened if I had been afforded the opportunities to partner with colleagues in the field years ago in the same manner I do today. There is a sense of regret that I did not have that level of support earlier but also excitement that there has been such progress in the field through organizations that exist to empower HR professionals at all levels. One significant benefit to becoming involved regardless of where you are in your career path is that your network will expand and as it does, offers and requests to volunteer and serve in other areas abundantly increase.

I am humbled and amazed by the range of agencies that reach out to seek my involvement in their community work. My challenge now is to determine how much more I can add to my crowded calendar and still do my best work in my EVP role and for the organizations I partner with as a member or board officer. I have gladly said yes to joining the Rotary Club of Atlanta, which is one of the world's largest Rotary chapters with nearly 500 members. Each one is a leader in their field and committed to community service. Beyond the typical Rotary activities, our chapter is engaged in tackling complex problems that plague our city. For example, because Atlanta has unfortunately become a hub for human trafficking, our Rotary has established an Anti-Human Trafficking Task Force. It is challenging and invigorating to be part of such a dynamic cohort of exceptional civic influencers.

I also said yes when asked to become a board member for the local chapter of the American Heart Association, which boasts more than 35 million volunteers and supporters at the national level. The nonprofit has been at the forefront of advances in

Each time I am asked to volunteer in a new role, there is the temptation to say that I am far too busy to assist. While sometimes my calendar is truly too full for me to add another ongoing appointment, other times I find I am so fatigued by the work involved with serving that I begin to view further participation as a burden versus a blessing. I find the inspiring words of others help me regain my focus and motivation to continue being part of the effort to elevate those in need of a helping hand.

Love cannot remain by itself—it has no meaning. Love has to be put into action and that action is service.
Mother Teresa

The life of a man consists not in seeing visions and dreaming dreams, but in active charity and in willing service.
Henry Wadsworth Longfellow

It is more blessed to give than to receive.
Acts 20:35, English Standard Version

Life's persistent and most urgent question is 'What are you doing for others?'
Martin Luther King Jr.

The best way to find yourself is to lose yourself in the service of others.
Mahatma Gandhi

I have found that among its other benefits, giving liberates the soul of the giver.
Maya Angelou

We make a living by what we get. We make a life by what we give.
Winston Churchill

Those who are happiest are those who do the most for others.
Booker T Washington

No one is useless in this world who lightens the burdens of another.
Charles Dickens

Never doubt that small groups of thoughtful committed citizens can change the world. Indeed, it's the only thing that ever has.
Margaret Mead

The greatness of a community is most accurately measured by the compassionate actions of its members.
Coretta Scott King

diagnosing, treating, and preventing heart disease since its establishment in 1924. For three years I was also a member of the Goodwill of North Georgia board, serving as chair of the compensation committee and later as vice chair after having been recruited to join that leadership team. The work reminded me of my father's volunteer efforts, as Goodwill's mission includes helping individuals prepare for a career through training and then finding employment. Also a nonprofit organization, Goodwill serves millions annually around the world.

I continue to draw upon my experience and apply my expertise while currently serving on the governing board of the Woodruff Arts Center in Atlanta. My involvement came through a nomination and interview process that ended with my accepting the position as chair of the compensation and HR committee. I am passionate about the arts and consider it a privilege to partner in ongoing efforts to enrich lives through performances and exhibitions offered by the Alliance Theatre, Atlanta Symphony Orchestra, and High Museum of Art. I am equally enthused to serve as board chair of 21st Century Leaders, another nonprofit agency that I became involved with by invitation. This organization exists to guide, train, and encourage young people so that they have the leadership skills required to overcome racial and class barriers. More than 1,600 high school students are served annually with programs and activities that expose their potential and fuel their passion.

The Georgia chapter of the International Women's Forum (IWF) is my remaining current board position and one I am especially proud to hold because of the organization's rich history and broad reach. IWF connects women who hold leadership positions around the world so that membership cuts across continents, cultures, and careers. A total of 33 nations are represented by the more than 5,000 women members, all of whom are selected by invitation. Georgia's chapter was established in 1988 with former U.S. First Lady Rosalynn Carter and Civil Rights Leader Coretta Scott King—Martin Luther King Jr.'s widow—among the founding members. One highlight of IWF membership is the opportunity to gain an international perspective and network through conferences that are held in different countries annually, creating an invaluable cultural experience.

The most recent developmental and volunteer initiative I have been a part of is Leadership Atlanta, which is a nine-month program for an annual cohort of approximately 80 executives who are chosen from the metro area through a nomination and application process. I was honored to be selected as part of the 2024 class that represented a broad cross-section of leaders from industries and agencies. We met monthly for full-day retreats, seminars, service projects, community tours, discussion groups, and work sessions within study groups that focused on resolving critical community issues.

Topics ranged from enriching education to improving public transportation and reforming healthcare, with each area examined through a racial lens. Having completed the intense training, I now have a clearer understanding of how the county and city intersect with corporations and businesses to meet community needs and how that triad can be fortified to do even more going forward. I am pleased that my involvement will continue, as I am one of 26 chosen from more than 4,000 alumni to serve as a study group facilitator for the incoming participants who will begin their work in 2025.

I anticipate functioning in that role will provide more unique opportunities for me to do what is undoubtedly the hardest work tied to serving in volunteer positions, namely continuing in the exercise of self-evaluation. Each membership, board appointment, and task assignment ultimately leads to moments where I am left contemplating what I can add to the effort at hand. I want to use the knowledge I have gleaned from the classroom to the boardroom to benefit others. I honestly ask and answer why I desire to be involved so that my motives stay pure. In addition, I review how my personal and professional priorities align with the work I am doing to ensure I am putting my energy into areas where I can be of most assistance. As I partner with leaders who sharpen me, hold me accountable, and challenge me to continue investing in others, I am indeed the one who is richly blessed. I experience the exhilarating joy of using my voice to empower others.

LESSONS LEARNED

The adage that you can't take it with you is a sobering truth. A U-Haul will never join a funeral procession. The possessions gathered throughout a lifetime are divided or disposed of when a loved one dies, just as the accolades for all the positions held and achievements celebrated during a career fade. What remains are the memories from precious moments that are inevitably a reflection of time invested in caring for others. Consider again the wise words of Maya Angelou who succinctly summarized the essence of a life well lived when she stated, "I've learned that people will forget what you said, people will forget what you did, but people will never forget how you made them feel."

For those individuals who have not had the joy of service and giving modeled through family traditions or for some other reason are hesitant to take on more responsibility as a volunteer,

I emphasize the reality that such work changes the lives of others while creating opportunities for personal and professional growth that are often unexpected and invaluable. This was certainly my experience as I became involved in working with my alma mater, UGA. I anticipated attending events where I could share my journey with students, but I never envisioned they would be teaching me how to prepare for a Ted Talk.

I was nominated, interviewed, and given a topic after I was selected to take the stage for a presentation. I first completed a six-week course that included students and faculty helping me understand that such a talk differs markedly from the speeches I typically deliver without qualms. I came to realize that a Ted Talk is incredibly stressful. That experience was in fact so intense that I never intend to do another one! But I learned a new skill and gained additional insight about myself as a public speaker so that I can honestly say I have no regrets.

Another positive tied to pursuing volunteer positions is the opportunity they provide to hone a professional skill or gain experience in a leadership role. There is often a frustration tied to the inability to grow in a current job for myriad reasons, from just beginning in a field and consequently feeling slotted at the entry-level to being sabotaged by office peers who fight for every promotion. Seek volunteer work as a way to overcome such obstacles. Choose an organization that aligns with your passion and actively engage in areas where you want to learn, be it serving on a financial committee or jumping into event planning. You will build your confidence, grow your network, and seize a competitive advantage. You will acquire both the skills and track record necessary to continue climbing the corporate ladder.

As you become actively engaged as a volunteer and public servant, you will undoubtedly realize the personal satisfaction that comes from seeing others reach a goal or overcome a struggle. The joy that accompanies such success is invigorating and results in a desire to become even more engaged in serving. Realize the need to guard your sanity by establishing boundaries. There will likely come a time when even though your calendar is full, you will continue to ponder every opportunity that becomes available because the work sounds intriguing, is tied to an important cause, or a person in your inner circle is the one asking for your assistance. Learn to say no. You must find a healthy balance to your schedule so that your loved ones are not ignored, your work performance does not slump, and the contributions you make to a cause are your best effort. You never want to be that person who adds the community title without doing the work. If you cannot manage the load and make a difference, do not take on the responsibility.

At the same time, do not use a busy schedule as an excuse to pass on every opportunity to become involved in work that lifts up others, be it as a mentor, board member, or leader of an initiative to solve a recurring community problem. Find a way to say yes at some point if for no other reason than to recognize the assistance you have received throughout your own journey. Others invested in you with the expectation and hope that you would in turn extend a helping hand to those who can benefit from your time and expertise. Continue that legacy of giving and assisting as a demonstration of your gratitude to those who have provided you support and guidance. Consider your service a thank you to those who opened doors on your behalf.

11

NAVIGATING FORWARD WITH
AN ATTITUDE OF GRATITUDE

A NALOGIES, METAPHORS, AND SIMILES ABOUND AS DESCRIPTORS FOR understanding the complexities of life, as well as how to maximize the years we are given. Advice is voiced in phrases that are so common they often become part of our vocabulary as children and persist into adulthood as ideas so familiar they are rarely contemplated despite the wisdom they convey. *Don't put all your eggs into one basket. Laughter is the best medicine. Every cloud has a silver lining. Actions speak louder than words. The early bird gets the worm. Never judge a book by its cover. No man is an island. Don't cast your pearls before swine. You reap what you sow. A bird in the hand is worth two in the bush. Where there's a will there's a way. Two heads are better than one. If at first you don't succeed, try, try again.*

There is also the familiar adage that urges us all to stop and smell the roses, which is advice I admit I have failed to faithfully follow. I realized while writing this book that for much of my career, I have lived my life with a focus on the growing list of demands at home and in the office, the need to build my knowledge base and network, the responsibilities assigned in expanding volunteer roles, as well as the endlessly tiring task of always being prepared for the day while planning the next best step for tomorrow. While I have embraced the attitude of the optimist who deems the glass to be half full and practiced the positive mindset that comes from always counting my blessings, I have rarely paused to engage in the level of deep reflection that has occurred as I have put the details of my journey on the printed page.

Looking in the proverbial rearview mirror at all that has transpired throughout my life has been a draining yet rejuvenating experience. There has been a level of angst as I follow my own advice and speak with courage about my experiences in Corporate America. I have relived painful moments and felt anew stinging emotions ranging from insecurity to vulnerability while recalling tough times during a marriage that failed, a graduate program that made me question my abilities, and work environments where I endured attacks that momentarily convinced me I was destined for defeat. I have grimaced with each vivid recollection of scenarios that made me once again battle the dreaded imposter syndrome and the effort required to quell all the doubts it creates. I have thankfully also felt the joy that comes from once again contemplating achievements that at one time were assumed to be impossible goals, as well as an enormous sense of appreciation and humility with the renewed realization of how many individuals have richly invested in me.

At every stage of my life, I have been buoyed by supportive family members, skilled mentors, and valued colleagues. They created the firm foundation I needed to continue learning, growing, and sharpening my skill set. The safety net they graciously created resulted in my ability to complete an amazing international assignment. They consistently provided wisdom while giving me both the courage and encouragement needed to learn through every lesson, overcome every obstacle, and persevere despite the inevitable challenges and frequent pain that come with growth. They are the reason I was able to break through the cement ceiling and unlock professional doors, as they kept me steady and strong through seasons of tumultuous change, always giving me the confidence to seize the next opportunity.

The path to the C-Suite required that I accept and manage change in all aspects of my life, beginning at an early age when I learned the value of determination and flexibility. Relocating from the Midwest to the South while still completing my high school education was the first significant shift I experienced. During that season of growth I gained the perspective of living life as a free agent, which served me well for all that was yet to come. There were frequent transitions as I finished my undergraduate education, started my career, and then diverted back to the collegiate experience to complete the MBA. Shortly after earning my master's degree, I adjusted to the new normal of married life. Change persisted as I attempted to make the relationship work while pursuing a Ph.D., despite being labeled "Ice Princess" by my spouse and warned regularly by faculty that I did not have the dedication to complete the doctorate.

I continued to shift places of employment as opportunities arose so that I could provide for my family as it grew. Taking on the role of motherhood with the addition of two sons was another enormous life event, as was ending a marriage that was destined to fail. I became a single mom burdened with significant and unexpected debt that mandated yet more change. Living and working abroad took the concept of change to an unnerving new level, as did the professional opportunities that existed upon my return. As a result of my experiences and determination, my talents and hard work, and an extensive network I developed through the years, I was able to advance in my career to the role of CHRO prior to reaching my current position as EVP/Chief Culture Officer.

Being a part of the executive leadership team for a Major League Baseball team was never an opportunity I envisioned while progressing as an HR professional. In fact, each advancement in my career to a new position of higher status and greater responsibilities resulted from an opportunity that I was made aware of through my network at a time when I was not actively seeking a change in employment. Each job has prepared me for my current work overseeing Braves' communications, community affairs, and people capital initiatives for nearly 500 employees and an additional 2,000 part-time ushers, food vendors, and game-day staff. I have gained knowledge and confidence, as well as unexpected moments of celebration.

There have been myriad changes that I have witnessed or helped implement throughout my decades in HR. I quickly realized that chaos is all too often a close companion to change, especially in a field such as Human Resources that has evolved and become more complex over time. I have certainly endured chaotic seasons as I pushed to implement advancements within an organization or as a result of the shifting paradigm within HR as a profession. I am truly grateful for the opportunities I

I often turn to literature and music when struggling to maintain a positive attitude or during those moments I find myself feeling more prone to speaking complaints than expressing gratitude. The following poem by an unknown author succinctly conveys the perspective I have maintained throughout my professional journey, especially when faced with obstacles.

Be thankful that you don't already have everything you desire,
 If you did, what would there be to look forward to?

Be thankful when you don't know something,
 For it gives you the opportunity to learn.

Be thankful for the difficult times.
 During those times you grow.

Be thankful for your limitations,
 Because they give you opportunities for improvement.

Be thankful for each new challenge,
 Because it will build your strength and character.

Be thankful for your mistakes.
 They will teach you valuable lessons.

Be thankful when you're tired and weary,
 Because it means you've made a difference.

It is easy to be thankful for the good things.
 A life of rich fulfillment comes to those who are
 also thankful for the setbacks.

have been given to advocate and implement changes that have advanced the field. The work has been rewarding yet exhausting, especially as a Black woman who is among the small percentage to take a seat in the C-Suite. Even after arriving, I have too often still had to fight to be heard and consequently know the level of fatigue that sets in as a result. I have become frustrated, fed up, and fired up throughout my career when I felt others were working to silence my voice or thwart my progress.

I find myself increasingly impatient as I see areas where more can be done to elevate and maximize the Human Resources function in Corporate America so that companies invest in their people capital, which is one reason I gladly accept invitations to speak at professional events across the country. I feel fortunate to have the opportunity to increasingly be a voice for change, especially at this point in my career. I have been reminded while reflecting on my journey of the times I wanted to question the norms but did not have the strength, wisdom, or experience to even know how to begin pushing for a new perspective within the profession.

There were plenty of times I felt defeated as I envisioned elevating the mission of my HR team, yet found I was relegated to continuing to function at the reactionary or fundamental level of completing immediate tasks instead of participating in planning for the future. Persistence and patience have continued to serve me well, however, as I am now an integral part of the team engaged in decision-making conversations that result in action plans. My voice is heard as I contribute to building strategies that maximize the power and potential of employees.

Reflecting on the level of evolution within the profession makes me grateful for the opportunities I have had to play a role in demanding and delivering change. There is enormous satisfaction in contemplating the challenges I faced, the courage I displayed, and the growth I have experienced while pushing myself and my field to do better. There are still times of aggravation as I see more that I believe can and should be done to improve the HR function and elevate employees, yet I am feeling very fulfilled and incredibly blessed.

I am convinced yet again that each chapter of my story has been integral to my ability to arrive in the C-Suite. Each setback and every disappointment became integral to gaining perspective and knowledge. Each failure was motivation to persevere and each frustration the symptom of growing pains. I would not have become a voice in the profession but for all that has transpired. Everything I experienced prepared me for where I am today and who I have become. I consequently embrace every aspect of my journey with an attitude of gratitude, including my personal peaks and valleys.

Granted, that was not what I was feeling during the seven years it took me to complete my doctorate. The memory of harsh words from faculty who were predicting my failure still stings today. I admittedly was not expressing such positive sentiments as I watched my marriage decline and ultimately dissipate in divorce. But I recognize the blessings that are tied to such seasons of heartache. My two sons, who are an integral part of my life, would not be here if not for my first marriage. That failed relationship is what makes me realize the extraordinary love I have found and cherish in my current marriage with Leon, who I met through another colleague while working for the media conglomerate.

Leon is the one who has understood my drive since the day we were introduced and consistently pushes me to go harder, do better, and reach my potential. We met just before my departure for Hong Kong and quickly developed a strong professional connection. As vice president of a staffing company, he was initially another person I was pleased to add to my network. It was not long before our relationship evolved into a romance more amazing than anything I could have envisioned for myself. At the time of our marriage in 2017, we became a blended family of three sons who have as strong a bond as the one Leon and I share with them and each other. He provides unwavering support and unending encouragement regardless of what I endeavor, including the writing of this book. It was his continual prompting of me to tell my story as another way to empower others that forced me to pursue and realize my long-held dream of becoming an author.

With Leon leading in my personal life such a strong team of supportive loved ones that includes my three sons and parents, I continue to be blessed beyond measure. The firm foundation I began to build on because of my family as a child remains firmly in place and elevates me as an adult. I have remarkable individuals in my life who applaud my success and are quick to assert I am capable of accomplishing more, suggesting for example, that I consider climbing to the next rung on the professional ladder and become a CEO. I can certainly envision accomplishing more within Corporate America in the years ahead. I also recognize there are equally challenging options in the realm of education, be it on a college campus or creating curriculum for corporate training. Opportunities to do more in advancing organizations, agencies, and causes that help others also abound and remain a priority as I contemplate what tomorrow will bring.

I do not know the storyline for my next life chapter, but I am convinced there are three certainties with regard to my future. One is that I know I have much more to learn regardless of what positions I may hold going forward. There will always be someone to provide new insights, an initiative to create new challenges, and an avenue to continue my growth as an individual and a professional. I also know that I will never embrace the idea of retiring. That word is not in my vocabulary. There will always be another void I can work to fill, another problem I can help resolve, and another person who needs a helping hand. This truth leads me to my third conviction, which is a statement I have hanging in my office: *Somewhere someone is looking for exactly what you have to offer.* Believing in that truth empowers me to eagerly anticipate what lies ahead and believe the best is yet to be. The words have never failed me but rather, instilled the courage and confidence I have needed to keep knocking on doors throughout my life. I did not stop until they opened, and I took my place in the C-Suite.

LESSONS LEARNED

Throughout the months of contemplation that were essential while writing this book, another adage consistently came to my mind. I was often reminded of the words from the fictional Hollywood character Forrest Gump, who wisely stated "Life is like a box of chocolates. You never know what you're going to get." My journey exemplifies the truth of that statement, as I could never have plotted or imagined the experiences and opportunities that were ahead when I started in my first HR job in 1997.

Much of what has occurred since involved a surprise element, sometimes with a negative result but more often with a pleasant outcome. I would venture to speculate that there are few individuals who have followed the exact path they charted while still in their youth. I am also convinced that it is the unexpected turns and twists in everyone's life that add adventure and excitement, as well as memorable moments never anticipated. There can also be overwhelming emotions of angst, anger, or sorrow when what is anticipated or desired does not develop.

Such feelings are magnified when there is an intentional slight involved that prevents the positive outcome that appeared to be within reach. Failure can be crushing regardless of what caused the downfall. I have learned that the best way to endure such disappointment is to embrace the moment regardless of the circumstances. This is not to say that it is easy to rebound after being pushed down or deflated, be it by an individual or a situation beyond control.

I hope that in candidly sharing my story, I have made it apparent that I know from my experiences the struggle is real and often seems endless. The message I want to make clear, however, is that every struggle and setback along with each success delivers a life lesson that is vital in building you for the moment at hand as well as your future. Embrace what you are enduring with the confidence you are being sharpened and readied for what comes next.

Regardless of where you are in your life or career, take a calculated moment to pause and reflect on where you have been and what you have accomplished. There is a healthy perspective gained by contemplating the struggles encountered, failures survived, knowledge gained, and successes achieved. Recognize those who have believed in you and whose words of wisdom or encouragement have given you the momentum needed to go forward in your daily life and on your professional path.

Take additional time to pause and consider the individuals you have encountered and empowered as a mentor. You will experience renewed strength and confidence as you realize all you have endeavored and endured, as well as your impact in the life of a person or the success of an organization. Express gratitude as you ponder your past, but do not linger too long focusing on yesterday. Remember that the purpose of the rearview mirror is to briefly look at where you have been and assess what is behind you. Its main purpose is to enable you to safely navigate the road ahead. It is imperative that you keep moving forward and as you do, always keep your eye on the next door that you want to open.

CONCLUSION

USING *YOUR* VOICE

I AM CONVINCED THAT THERE IS A DEVIL AND THERE IS A GOD. THE DEVIL has his legion of people doing evil and God has His angels who partner with saints here on earth to be the light in this world. I would say I am unwavering in my decision to stand firm on God's team, which is no doubt how I survived dealing with the devil's attacks on a frequent basis as I steadily rose through the ranks within the field of Human Resources. I also have no qualms stating with certainty that myriad others have engaged in such battles while navigating their own career path as they faced down false critics, circumvented conniving oppressors, and rose above all determined to plot their demise. I have found the fight especially exhausting given I am one in the minuscule cohort of Black women to persevere until arriving in Corporate America's C-Suite.

Perseverance is in fact one of two words I use to identify myself, with the other being courage. My goal in all that I attempt as a wife, mother, daughter, friend, volunteer, mentor, or executive in a leadership position is to maintain the courage to have the perseverance necessary to always move forward. My purpose in picking up the proverbial pen and writing this book is to provide insights that will empower others to do the same, all while emphasizing the heartache and headaches I have encountered while achieving success and living my purpose. I have not sugar-coated my experiences because I want others who are struggling with imposter syndrome, inequities stemming from race or gender, microaggressions, or self-doubt fueled by naysayers to stay strong and be encouraged.

Strength comes from knowing yourself and remaining true to your identity regardless of what is transpiring in your home or within the workplace. It is a trait displayed when refusing to be pulled down or led astray by an attacker or negative situation, choosing instead to protect your brand by refraining, retreating, and re-evaluating as a strategy for avoiding behavior that equates to self-sabotage. The strength required for such a measured response during a season of doubt, frustration, or perhaps even fury is bolstered by building a strong foundation that exists through relationships established and nurtured among family members and beyond.

Include colleagues, mentors, and an inner circle of trusted friends in your network, always carefully trusting only those who will speak truth to you with the confidence you will use the constructive criticism to continue climbing the corporate ladder and ultimately shatter the cement ceiling. Such a team will result in partnerships necessary for you to mature as a leader prepared for challenges that often arrive wrapped in chaos, provide unexpected opportunities for growth, and bolster within you the determination to be a voice that calls for change.

I am passionate about the importance of voice, which is why the theme of finding the courage to speak is incorporated into the title of this book and has been a message conveyed throughout each chapter. I readily recognize and admit that I have kept quiet at times when struggling to overcome a lack of confidence or reeling from battered self-esteem. For far too long, I was incapable of verbalizing what I was experiencing as my first marriage was dissolving, my doctoral program spiraled into a deflating endeavor, and I deflected attacks by female colleagues early in my career. As a result, I felt as if I was a failure because I allowed myself to be diminished by remaining silent.

Thankfully the outcome as I walked through such stressful seasons was ultimately positive as I became intent on engaging in self-examination and contemplation that often made me realize I was not where I belonged, be it as a spouse or employee. I learned that failure is not a destination but a time of transition. For me, the shift from feeling defeated to moving forward inevitably occurred as I evaluated what I needed to thrive, where I wanted to engage to be a positive force in my career and community, what knowledge I needed to acquire to reach my goals, and most importantly how to tune out negative voices.

My mantra became the truth that what people say about me and how they judge me is none of my business. I put my energy into improving my skills, building my brand, and embracing each experience with the knowledge it was making me stronger for what was yet to come in my personal life and profession. That mindset empowered me to envision myself as a free agent always ready and able to soar. I also renewed my commitment to do more for others, be it as a transformational leader in my executive position, a mentor to a young person beginning their career, or a community volunteer determined to help lift a burden by meeting a need.

Each change in position brought challenges and successes that increased my confidence and strengthened my voice. Each invitation to serve or partner in an initiative expanded my reach to a larger audience. I am now gratefully positioned to speak more boldly and broadly for change that I deem is imperative not only within Human Resources but for individuals, communities, corporations, and our nation as a whole.

My message is that DEI must be seen as more than a politically correct agenda item included in a strategic plan, but rather be prioritized as a means to create racial equity that is needed to empower individuals and elevate all of society. We must be intentional and specific about initiatives, activities, and programming that makes every individual feel welcome within their neighborhood, school, and workplace.

My message is that women, and especially women of color, need to have opportunities to reach their potential regardless of the career path they pursue. Women belong in the C-Suite and will rise to that executive level more readily if they are actively sponsored and mentored by men in positions of power who must speak up and do more to open doors.

I also have a message targeted specifically at women who must come together as a united force of talent that cannot be overlooked or circumvented. Positive change will be inevitable when women unite to stand on each other's shoulders. We must move beyond the paranoia, hostility, and competition that is now the norm and instead commit to lifting each other up.

My message is that more individuals need to find their voice and develop the courage to use it for the benefit of themselves and others. While I have written primarily about changes I deem vital for the future of Corporate America and how I have used my voice in my professional role, I am convinced that each of us is responsible for ensuring that we as a society and nation are moving forward. That requires we unite and speak in unison for paradigm shifts that will empower the weak, elevate the downtrodden, expose the unjust, and embolden leaders to make hard decisions despite the outcry from those who object. Imagine the positive energy that will result when voices calling for positive change are heard. Now imagine that the impetus begins with you.

My message to you is to do the work to discover your identity, your passions, and your purpose. Build the network you need to fortify your confidence and self-esteem so that you are capable of facing whatever challenges surface going forward. Embrace each situation as training for what comes next and commit to living with an attitude of gratitude for each person who has walked alongside you throughout your journey. Honor their investment in you by mentoring those who are seeking guidance as they embark on their career.

Most importantly, find your voice and learn how to use it. Begin by standing up as your own advocate when necessary, which will strengthen your resolve to be a voice for others as well. Note that it is important to be strategic as to when you speak, the message you deliver, and the way in which you share your thoughts. Just as a musician relies on modulation for emphasis during a performance, know when to speak softly as well as how to engage in fierce conversation. Realize there are indeed times where silence is best, so learn to be comfortable with the quiet.

As you become more emboldened and increasingly outspoken, you will see the impact of your words that have the power to spark action. You will observe firsthand the fact that courage of voice is indeed a powerful key that will unlock professional doors, not only for yourself but others.

RESOURCES

F OLLOWING IS A LIST OF WORKS BY SOME AUTHORS ON MY BOOKSHELF at home and in my office that I always reference. I share these titles with you as a source of encouragement and empowerment.

Art Barter: *The Art of Servant Leadership II: How You Get Results Is More Important Than the Results Themselves*

Brene' Brown: *Atlas of the Heart: Mapping Meaningful Connection and the Language of Human Experience*

Brene' Brown: *Dare to Lead: Brave Work. Tough Conversations. Whole Hearts.*

Brene' Brown: *The Gifts of Imperfection*

Jennifer Brown: *How to be an Inclusive Leader: Your Role in Creating Cultures of Belonging Where Everyone Can Thrive*

Jim Collins: *Good to Great: Why Some Companies Make the Leap... And Others Don't*

Jim Collins & Jerry I. Porras: *Built to Last: Successful Habits of Visionary Companies*

Amy Cuddy: *Presence: Bringing your Boldest Self to your Biggest Challenges*

Robin Diangelo: *Nice Racism: How Progressive White People Perpetuate Racial Harm*

BJ Gallagher & Warren H. Schmidt: *A Peacock in the Land of Penguins: A Fable about Creativity & Courage*

Bill George with Peter Sims: *True North: Discover your Authentic Leadership*

Marshall Goldsmith & Mark Reiter: *The Earned Life: Lose Regret, Choose Fulfillment*

Minda Harts: *The Memo: What Women of Color Need to Know to Secure a Seat at the Table*

Pat Heim, Ph.D. & Susan A. Murphy, Ph.D., MBA, with Susan K. Golant: *In the Company Women: Indirect Aggression Among Women: Why We Hurt Each Other and How to Stop*

Sally Helgesen and Marshall Goldsmith: *How Women Rise: Break the 12 Habits Holding You Back from Your Next Raise, Promotion, or Job*

Rachel Hollis: *Girl, Stop Apologizing: A Shame-Free Plan for Embracing and Achieving Your Goals*

John P. Kotter: *Leading Change*

Ancella B. Livers & Keith A. Caver: *Leading in Black and White: Working Across the Racial Divide in Corporate America*

Susan MacKenty Brady: *Mastering Your Inner Critic and 7 Other High Hurdles to Advancement: How the Best Women Leaders Practice Self-Awareness to Change What Really Matters*

Steve McClatchy: *Decide: Work Smarter, Reduce Your Stress, and Lead by Example*

Jennifer McCollum: *In Her Own Voice: A Woman's Rise to CEO: Overcoming Hurdles to Change the Face of Leadership*

Pat Mitchell: *Becoming a Dangerous Woman: Embracing Risk to Change the World*

Randal Pinkett & Jeffrey Robinson with Philana Patterson: *Black Faces in White Places: 10 Game-Changing Strategies to Achieve Success and Find Greatness*

Dr. Cheryl Polote-Williamson: *Affirmed Volume II: 365 Days of Positive Thoughts and Actions to Start Your Day (Vol. 2)*

Dr. Cheryl Polote-Williamson: *The Art of Influence: Inviting Success into Every Area of Your Life*

Quotabelle: *Beautifully Said: Quotes by Remarkable Women and Girls Designed to Make You Think*

Dr. Randy Ross: *Relationomics: Business Powered by Relationships*

Sheryl Sandberg: *Lean In: Women, Work, and the Will to Lead*

Kim Scott: *Radical Candor: How to Get What You Want by Saying What You Mean*

Susan Scott: *Fierce Conversations: Achieving Success at Work & in Life, One Conversation at a Time*

Ella Bell Smith, Stella M. Nkomo, et al.: *Our separate ways: Black and White Women and the Struggle for Professional Identity*

Susan Steinbrecher & Joel Bennett, Ph.D.: *Heart-Centered Leadership: Lead Well, Live Well*

Susan Steinbrecher & Robert Schaefer, Ph.D.: *Meaningful Alignment: Mastering Emotionally Intelligent Interactions at Work and in Life*

Dr. Suess: *Oh, the Places You'll Go!*

Beverly Daniel Tatum: *Why Are All the Black Kids Sitting Together in the Cafeteria?: And Other Conversations About Race*

Dr. Kecia Thomas: *Diversity Dynamics in the Workplace*

Judith Turnock & Price Cobbs: *Cracking the Corporate Code: The Revealing Success Stories of 32 African-American Executives.*

Adrien Katherine Wing, Editor: *Critical Race Feminism: A Reader*

CITATIONS

Alcom, C. (22 February, 2021). "Black women executives making history in the C-Suite offer career advice to those following in their footsteps. *CNN Business.* Retrieved February 20, 2024, from https://www.cnn.com/2021/02/20/business/black-women-c-suite-executives/index.html

Browne, S. (2017) *HR on Purpose: Developing Deliberate People Passion.* Society For Human Resource Management.

Catalyst. (1 February, 2023). "Women of color in the United States (QuickTake)." *Catalyst: Workplaces that Work for Women.* Retrieved January 10, 2024, from https://www.catalyst.org/research/women-of-color-in-the-united-states

Cobbs, P. M., & Turnock, J. L. (2003). *Cracking the corporate code: The revealing success stories of 32 African-American executives.* Washington DC: Amacom.

Colletta, J. (1 April, 2021). "Number of the day: DEI after George Floyd." Human Resource Executive. Retrieved

May 17, 2024, from https://hrexecutive.com/number-of-the-day-dei-after-george-floyd

Decision Lab. (No Date). The Butterfly Effect. Retrieved February 29, 2024, from https://thedecisionlab.com/reference-guide/economics/the-butterfly-effect

ExpatLiving. (22 February, 2023). "25 fun facts about Hong Kong." Retrieved March 2, 2024, from https://expatliving.hk/25-fun-facts-about-hong-kong

Giscombe, K., & Mathis, M.C. (2002). "Leveling the playing field for women of color in corporate management: Is the business case enough?" *Journal of Business Ethics* 37(1), 103-119.

Groysberg, B., Kelly, K., & MacDonald, B. (March 2011). "The new path to the C-Suite." *Harvard Business Review*. Retrieved March 2, 2024, from https://hbr.org/2011/03/the-new-path-to-the-c-suite

Gur, T. (No date). "Who is Maya Angelou?" *Elevate Society*. Retrieved March 1, 2024, from https://elevatesociety.com/maya-angelou/

Hong Kong Chartered Governance Institute. (11 May, 2023). "Diversity, equity and inclusion (DEI)." *CGJ*. Retrieved March 13, 2024, from https://cgj.hkcgi.org.hk/diversity-equity-and-inclusion-dei

Inman, P. (1998). "Women's career development at the glass ceiling." In L.L. Bierema (Ed.), *Women's career development across the lifespan: Insights and strategies for women, organizations, and adult educators*. New Directions for Adult and Continuing Education, No.80. San Francisco: Jossey-Bass.

McGlauflin, P. (2 May, 2024). "How HR chiefs went from 'lepers' to C-Suite power players." Fortune. Retrieved May 17, 2024, from https://fortune.com/2024/05/02/hr-chief-new-c-suite-power-player/

McLean & Company. (2024). HR Trends Report 2024: What HR Trends are Making Waves in 2024? Retrieved May 1, 2024, from https://hr.mcleanco.com/research/ss/hr-trends-report-2024

Mishra, A. (12 March, 2024). 100+ Common Proverbs with Meaning and Examples. Retrieved April 30, 2024, from https://leverageedu.com/blog/common-proverbs/

NNRoad. (19 June, 2023). "Decoding the Vibrant Work Culture in Hong Kong: Insights & Trends." Retrieved March 11, 2024, from https://nnroad.com/blog/work-culture- in-hong-kong

Nagashybayeva, G. (November 2023). "Globalization: A Resource Guide." Library of Congress. Retrieved March 1, 2024, from https://guides.loc.gov/globalization

Obama, M. (25 July, 2016). "Remarks by the First Lady at the Democratic National Convention." Retrieved March 1, 2024, from https://obamawhitehouse.archives.gov/the-press-office/2016/07/25/remarks-first-lady-democratic-national-convention

Ramirez, J. (24 May, 2021). "One year after George Floyd's death, what's changed for HR?" Human Resource Executive. Retrieved May 15, 2024, from https://hrexecutive.com/-one-year-after-george-floyds-death-whats-changed-for-hr

Sandberg, S. (2013). *Lean In: Women, Work, and the Will to Lead*. New York: Knopf Doubleday Publishing Group.

Saxe, J. G. (1872). "The Blind Men and the Elephant." Retrieved March 8, 2024, from https://allpoetry.com/The-Blind-Man-And-The-Elephant

Thomas, K.M. (2005). *Diversity dynamics in the workplace.* Belmont: Thomson Wadsworth.

U.S. Department of Commerce, Economics & Statistics Administration, U.S. Census Bureau (2002). "The Black Population in the United States: March 2002." Retrieved January 23, 2005, from http://www.census.gov/prod/2003pubs/p20-541.pdf

Voepel, M. (12 July, 2006). "Albright empowers all-decade team at luncheon." ESPN.com. Retrieved March 6, 2024, from https://www.espn.com/wnba/columns/story?columnist=voepel_mechelle&id=2517642

Wing, A. (2003). Introduction. In Wing, A.K, (Ed.) *Critical Race Feminism.* (2nd Ed.). 1-19. New York: New York University Press.

Workday, Inc. (2023). Global CHRO AI Indicator Report: A Vision for Strategic Value. Retrieved May 14, 2024, from https://criticaleye.com/inspiring/insights-servfile.cfm?-id=6486

ABOUT THE AUTHOR

DERetta Rhodes is a vision-driven executive who has broad experience in strategic planning and Human Resources spanning multiple industries including professional services, media, financial services, and nonprofits. DeRetta has been a leader in Diversity, Equity, and Inclusion (DEI) initiatives long before it became a business imperative. As a result, DeRetta was recently recognized at the Sports Inclusion Conference by winning the top National Diversity & Leadership Top 100 HR Professionals Award (2023) and Georgia Titan 100 (2024). DeRetta has been recognized three years in a row as a 100 Women of Influence by *Atlanta Business Chronicle* and received the Oncon Icon Award Top 100 Human Resources Professionals two consecutive years.

DeRetta is an active volunteer in the community and brings a broad set of capabilities and skills to several not-for-profit boards. She is the board chair for the 21st Century Leaders, a trustee member, governing board member and HR & Compensation Chair of the Woodruff Arts Center, to name a few of her roles. She is also a sought-after speaker in the areas of leadership;

women in leadership; diversity, equity, inclusion; and leadership development. She completed a Ted Talk (2018) titled "From Survive to Thrive: Women of Color in Corporate Leadership."

DeRetta received her Ph.D. in adult education from the University of Georgia, her Master's in Business Administration from Clark Atlanta University, and her undergraduate degree from the University of Georgia. DeRetta is a mother to three sons and lives with her husband, Leon, in Atlanta, Georgia.

FOLLOW DERETTA

LinkedIn: https://www.linkedin.com/in/deretta-cole-rhodes-phd
Instagram: @draecole
Facebook: Elevate Advisory Group

Photo Credit: Nick Nelson, BranPrenuer

Printed in the USA
CPSIA information can be obtained
at www.ICGtesting.com
LVHW010942120724
785245LV00002B/384

9 781961 863019